BFI Film Classics

The BFI Film Classics series introduces, interprets and celebrates landmarks of world cinema. Each volume offers an argument for the film's 'classic' status, together with discussion of its production and reception history, its place within a genre or national cinema, an account of its technical and aesthetic importance, and in many cases, the author's personal response to the film.

For a full list of titles in the series, please visit https://www.bloomsbury.com/uk/series/bfi-film-classics/

T0347690

In memory of Patricia Lovell (1929–2013)

Picnic at Hanging Rock

Anna Backman Rogers

THE BRITISH FILM INSTITUTE
Bloomsbury Publishing Plc
50 Bedford Square, London, WC1B 3DP, UK
1385 Broadway, New York, NY 10018, USA
29 Earlsfort Terrace, Dublin 2, Ireland

BLOOMSBURY is a trademark of Bloomsbury Publishing Plc

First published in Great Britain 2022 by Bloomsbury on behalf of the
British Film Institute
21 Stephen Street, London W1T 1LN
www.bfi.org.uk

The BFI is the lead organisation for film in the UK and the distributor of Lottery funds for film.
Our mission is to ensure that film is central to our cultural life, in particular by supporting and
nurturing the next generation of filmmakers and audiences. We serve a public role which covers
the cultural, creative and economic aspects of film in the UK.

Cover artwork: © Cathy Lomax
Series cover design: Louise Dugdale
Series text design: Ketchup/SE14
Images from *Picnic at Hanging Rock* (Peter Weir, 1975), Picnic Productions/BEF Film Distributors/
South Australian Film Commission/Australian Film Commission; *A Dream Within a Dream:
The Making of 'Picnic at Hanging Rock'* (Mark Hartley, 2004), Famous by Tuesday/Umbrella
Entertainment; *The Falling* (Carol Morley, 2014), © BFI/BBC/Malady Films Ltd; *Innocence* (Lucile
Hadzihalilovic, 2004), © Ex Nihilo/Bluelight L'École Ltd/UK Film Council/Les Ateliers de Baere/
Gimages/Love Streams; *The Virgin Suicides* (Sofia Coppola, 1999), © Virgin Suicides LLC

Bloomsbury Publishing Plc does not have any control over, or responsibility for, any third-party
websites referred to or in this book. All internet addresses given in this book were correct at the
time of going to press. The author and publisher regret any inconvenience caused if addresses
have changed or sites have ceased to exist, but can accept no responsibility for any such changes.

A catalogue record for this book is available from the British Library.

A catalog record for this book is available from the Library of Congress.

ISBN: PB: 9/8-1-8390-2335-4
        ePDF: 978-1-8390-2337-8
        ePUB: 978-1-8390-2336-1

Produced for Bloomsbury Publishing Plc by Sophie Contento
Printed and bound in India

To find out more about our authors and books visit www.bloomsbury.com
and sign up for our newsletters.

Contents

Acknowledgments

Thank you to Rebecca Barden at Bloomsbury for her enthusiastic support of this project, Angus Johnstone at NFSA, who went above and beyond to help me access archival interviews in the middle of the Covid-19 pandemic, Sophie Contento for her meticulous attention to detail, Bruce Smeaton for being a congenial correspondent, Ina Bertrand, Jennifer Lovell, Ingrid Weir and Martha Ansara, all of whom granted me permission to access important archival material. This book was written during my research leave over 2021, which was sponsored by the Swedish Riksbankens Jubileumsfond. I am very grateful to them for the financial support which gave me respite to research, to think and to write. My gratitude is also due to my dearest dad, Nigel, who forwarded a copy of Patricia Lovell's autobiography to me from Australia via express post, and – as always – to my girls, Olivia and Mia … who are, quite simply, everything.

1 Within a Dream: Origins, Production and Filming

Haunting … it seems that in writing on Peter Weir's *Picnic at Hanging Rock* (1975), one cannot help but invoke this at once nebulous, yet appropriate description of the film's aesthetic and affective force. For those viewers whom the film touches, this visually stunning cinematic experience that depicts a terrifying chasm or void of meaning leaves a trace of feeling within that is, in fact, commensurate with being haunted. This exquisite film, which in and of itself centres on themes of absence, longing and lack, also intimates a far more sinister reality: a violence done to young girls on the cusp of womanhood, the denial and disenfranchisement of Aboriginal people and their land, and the folly and arrogance of white, colonial, European settler culture held in place by pomp, ceremony and arcane ritual, all of which is only ever partially concealed by a beguiling, captivating carapace. This formal device that serves both to hold us at a studied distance – to keep us from *really* seeing – and to gesture towards that which we are not really seeing *is*, I contend, the very essence of *Picnic at Hanging Rock*. This double manoeuvre of acknowledgment and denial creates an ambivalence which is, in turn, crucial to the film's emotional range and register; it is, in fact, its objective correlative. That is, *Picnic* is a film of psychological terror that unfolds in the daylight; if one chooses to give in to it – a position into which the viewer is coaxed by the film itself – it subsists within the perceptive viewer for years afterwards. For if *Picnic* is a strikingly beautiful film, one must question what that beauty is being put in service of: what is it actually concealing from us? And, by extension, if *Picnic* haunts us, it is precisely *because* of that powerful undertow, *because* of the spectral absence we do not want to acknowledge, and yet which insistently returns to perturb us and to force us

into a reckoning with our own understanding of a reality that is
philosophical, psychological and necessarily political in nature.
This is why we keep returning to the Rock.

New Australian Cinema and the status of *Picnic*

Picnic is now considered by contemporary critics and scholars
to be exemplary of the so-called New Australian Cinema or AFC
Genre style of film-making – terms used retrospectively to describe
Australian cinema as a cultural product that was legislated into
existence in the late 1960s and early 1970s by Australia's then
prime minister, John Gorton.[1] Institutions such as a state-financed
film school and the Australian Film Development Corporation (the
predecessor to the Australian Film Commission and Screen Australia,
and henceforth known here as AFDC) sponsored the careers and
initial output of directors such as Bruce Beresford (whose 1977
film *The Getting of Wisdom* explores similar thematic – and
sapphic – territory to *Picnic*), Gillian Armstrong and Phillip Noyce.
Weir himself has described *Picnic* as 'a subsidized idea … the sort of
film that could only come out of the optimism of a new industry'.[2]
The films made during this period not only revolutionised the
Australian film industry, which had been beset by the popularity of
American and British cinematic imports, but also helped to introduce
Australian film to a global audience. However, the term AFC Genre
is not merely indicative of a particular industrial and state-sponsored
or facilitated relationship; the films that emerged from this period,
of which *Picnic* is prototypical, are renowned for their complex style
and thematic preoccupations with Australian land and identity.

In stark contrast to the popular 'ocker' comedy – a rather
priapic genre of film that centred on and problematically shored up
a specific notion of simple, rugged Australian masculinity – the AFC
Genre films reveal a fraught and dark nostalgia for an earlier period
in modern Australia's colonial history. Frequently based on literary
adaptation – the central themes and tenets of which are evoked
through meticulous production design – these films, in essence,
helped to establish an identifiable and distinctive form of national
cinema. It is neither surprising that *Picnic* in particular has become
so inextricably bound up with certain facets of Australian creative
production, nor remarkable that it continues to exert a profound

influence on the popular cultural imaginary that extends well beyond the boundaries of the southern hemisphere.

However, despite *Picnic*'s reputation as the quintessential example of this style of film-making (and the extent to which this may be true is contested), its success was neither assured nor expected at the time of its production and filming. Peter Weir, Cliff Green (screenwriter) and Patricia Lovell (executive producer) have all individually expressed in interview their surprise at the film's subsequent popularity.[3] Brian McFarlane notes that

[i]n 1975, in view of the success of the ocker comedies, a gently-paced, decorative mood piece, in which atmosphere mattered more than plot, could hardly have been expected to launch the 'serious' revival of Australian cinema; however, that is essentially what *Picnic at Hanging Rock* achieved.[4]

Picnic opened in Adelaide, South Australia, on 8 August 1975 at the Hindley Cinema Complex and met with widespread critical acclaim (as 'the first true masterpiece of the Australian cinema'[5]) and outstanding takings at the box office (over 5 million AUD, which was significant at the time for a film with a final budget of just over 443,000 AUD). *Picnic* was the third highest-grossing film in Australia in 1975 after *Jaws* (1975) and *The Towering Inferno* (1974). Yet this did not translate fluidly into critical awards; although nominated for seven awards by the Australian Film Institute in 1976, *Picnic* did not receive any, and the film's only significant accolades came in the form of a BAFTA for Russell Boyd's superb cinematography and an Australian Writers' Guild award for Cliff Green's sensitively adapted screenplay. The film did appear at several international film festivals, most notably at Cannes in 1976, but did not open in the US until 1979 (in fact, after the release of Weir's following feature film, *The Last Wave*, made in 1977). Both Weir and Lovell have stated that they had anticipated that the film's sustained ambivalence and lack of closure would be difficult to sell to an American audience; Lovell suggested that the infamous

director's cut (which is the rarest of things: a shorter version of the film by some seven minutes) was in fact already prepared by Weir at the time of the film's release specifically for an American audience;[6] that said, it is difficult to see how this would have been more satisfying to an audience supposedly so ill-equipped to deal with ambiguities, amplifying as it does the emotionally fractious state of the characters, evacuating the film's pacing of moments of release and catharsis so as to compound the central tragedy, and crucially, opening up the possibility that Mrs Appleyard may have murdered Sara Waybourne.[7]

Patricia Lovell and *Picnic's* pre-production phase

The film's shooting schedule was exceptionally tight (six weeks) and took place across several locations and states (Martindale Hall in the Clare Valley of South Australia, and Mount Macedon and Woodend in Victoria), but the film was in gestation for many years beforehand. Cardinal to the film's existence is its producer Patricia Lovell, who, in my view, has not been granted enough recognition for her assiduous determination to bring the film to life. Lovell had read and become fascinated by Joan Lindsay's original novel (published in 1967) and carried within her the dream of adapting it for the film screen for many years. In interview in 1993, she said:

I was mesmerised by it because it was the story of an alien land really. I understood this English thing because of my grandmother. This English thing of a school mistress in the height of the Australian summer putting young girls into black stockings and corsets – which is quite bizarre. And all this English tradition amongst this dangerous terrain … I mean, this is why there are so many problems now because no lessons were learned from the original people … they just decided to do all of this on European standards. It's so crazy and so desperate … To me, it wasn't a romantic story, *it was a horror story*. I just became fascinated by it and stayed fascinated by it. (emphasis mine)[8]

Here, Lovell evinces a keen sense of the particularity of the novel's location and timeframe. The narrative takes place one year before the process of federation by which Australia declared itself a united commonwealth. Jonathan Rayner has also duly noted that the 'milieu' of *Picnic* is one 'poised between the centenary of British settlement in 1888 and the federation of the colonized states in 1901'.[9] As such, Lovell recognised that Appleyard College is a vast and archaic Victorian institution that looms hellaciously over a land it symbolically claims or seeks to master in the name of civilisation with wilful disregard for its Aboriginal history and people. Both Mrs Appleyard and her college for 'young ladies' are vestiges of an empire that is on the verge of disintegration. For this vulgar pomposity, both mistress and college pay dearly in the novel (Mrs Appleyard dies by suicide and the college is engulfed by a bushfire). To capture not only the novel's inherent mystery, but also its deeply rooted violence, Lovell needed a director with a sensitivity towards and an aptitude for capturing the ephemeral and fleeting moments that come to define life, as well as its inevitable sadness. Lovell had seen Weir's previous short films *Michael* (1971) and *Homesdale* (1971) and felt that both had a 'marvellous sense of mystery' about them.[10] She also discerned Weir's 'capacity to see the unusual or sinister under every-day and normal events', which would be essential to conveying the baleful undercurrent of Lindsay's novel.[11]

Although markedly different in style and tone to *Picnic*, taken together all three films suggest a preoccupation with Australian Gothic themes, to which Lovell was also sensitised. She was certainly able to detect an artistic sensibility in Weir that would serve both the magnificence and the terror of Lindsay's story. She approached Weir (having interviewed him previously for the *Today* programme) in the latter part of 1972 with a copy of the book and expressed enthusiastic interest in developing the project with him.

At the time, Weir was working on his own original screenplay for a film that would eventually become *The Cars That Ate Paris* (1974) and professed to be, initially, uninterested. However, a mere two months later, he called Lovell late one evening to let her know he had just finished reading the novel and believed that it was something he desperately needed to make. Lovell had not secured the rights to Lindsay's book, and, perhaps more problematically, she did not have extensive experience as a producer at the time. Lovell, at this point in the narrative, was rather well-known as a long-standing host of the *Today* programme and various children's television programmes on Australia's Broadcasting Commission (ABC). Cliff Green (*Picnic*'s screenwriter) claims that Lovell had an extraordinarily difficult time trying to convince both the AFDC and the South Australian Film Corporation (SAFC) that not only a woman, but one with relatively little experience, was up to the formidable task of producing a film all by herself. Lovell confirms this in her autobiography, in which she sets out the details of her initial encounter with Nadine Hollow at the AFDC:

it was a great shock to be patronised by this woman who pointed out that I had no experience in this field. I countered that many first-time producers who had approached the AFDC had been encouraged (they were all men). It was the first time I came up against a woman in power who did not wish to see another woman achieve. (It's happened with boring regularity in my film career.) My application for development money was turned down.[12]

The antediluvian nature of the Australian film industry at the time clearly determined that even women (with access to power) must play by patriarchal rules in a game already rigged against their own success and achievements. Lovell decided that she would have to secure a producer's credit if she were to hold any sway with the AFDC and volunteered to produce, for no personal fee, a documentary film about the development of the new opera house in Sydney. The resulting film – *Monster or Miracle? Sydney Opera House* (1973), directed by Bruce Beresford – was made possible largely through Lovell's own contacts in the television industry. Nonetheless, the AFDC rejected her application for development funds once again, this time claiming that *Picnic* was 'too risky a subject' for them to sponsor.[13] However, she subsequently discovered this was a wholly fictitious claim, since the AFDC had offered 4,500 AUD to a production company wishing to develop a story about 'a band of children who disappeared in the Blue Mountains'. Armed with this information (which she had received from Moya Wood, Cliff Green's agent), Lovell demanded an explanation from the AFDC. She writes:

[t]here seemed to be a crack in the innocent façade presented so I pressed my point with the information that I would be reporting the matter to Joan Lindsay's publishers and literary agent, and that we would need to view immediately the synopsis of this original idea that had elicited this large sum [the Blue Mountains project]. I then stormed out ... I rang the following day to inform the AFDC to expect another application from me for script development and I was subsequently rewarded the grand sum of 1,500 AUD.[14]

However, Lovell's refusal to be intimidated by the vagaries and whims of a patriarchal industry would continue to be tested throughout the pre- and post-production periods of *Picnic*.

At this stage, she was still far from securing the requisite funds she needed to develop the film and remained open to the idea of co-production, due to her relative lack of experience; she thus acquiesced to Weir's suggestion that the producers currently attached to his own film *Cars* – Jim and Hal McElroy – come on board *Picnic*. There were critical problems with this arrangement from the outset, though, according to Lovell:

nonplussed that we had to take on two, I knew we had no option as the boys worked as a team. Immediately I was at a disadvantage. So far, this had been a personal endeavour and naively I believed that I would be an equal member of the team – instead I was in danger of becoming invisible. I respected the McElroys' ability and tough approach, and knew that because of their solid experience they would be an invaluable help in moving the film into production. But there was no way I would be pushed aside.[15]

This dynamic led to multiple clashes of opinion over the artistic direction of the film, since the McElroys, having read Green's second draft of the screenplay, wished to have the narrative reformulated as a 'lesbian romp' with 'commercial' appeal; as a result, Green and Lovell privately started referring to this proposed change in course as 'Carry on up The Rock'.[16] Although these suggested additions are evidently tasteless (and preposterous) – and would have markedly changed the tone of the film for the worse – it is intriguing that the McElroys were keen to heighten the latent homoerotic and sapphic undertones of Lindsay's original material as this has been a long-standing point of contention with regard to the film's sexual politics (a reading for which Weir himself is only willing to admit a margin of possibility) and to which I will return later in this book.[17] Nonetheless, Lovell confirms this disagreement over the direction of the film which nearly waylaid the pre-production entirely. She writes:

[a]rmed with Cliff's screenplay, we decided to approach the AFDC for part-production finance … the application was flatly turned down [again]. Hal and Jim McElroy called me to a meeting and let me know that my involvement in the project was a stumbling block and the film would work better for

them and the AFDC if changes were made to the script to make it more 'commercial'. They wanted to meet with Joan Lindsay and Cliff Green to discuss their ideas ... these ideas, which included some sexual innuendoes, would not only be frowned upon by Joan Lindsay, but could lose us the rights. Their vision then of the film was certainly not mine, nor Peter's. Our meeting took place as I was 'walked', a McElroy on either side, around Wentworth Park in Ultimo. After three laps it became apparent that they wanted me to move out and let them take over 'for the sake of the film'. On the fourth lap I suggested they move aside while I gave due consideration to what I believed was 'best for the sake of the film'. That afternoon, I had a call from the AFDC telling me that the McElroys had no confidence in the film and had resigned as co-producers. For the moment, Peter and I decided to continue on our own. Shortly afterwards, we met with the director of the AFDC, Tom Stacey, and the corporation's lawyer, Lloyd Hart ... for the first time their reaction to our proposed film was positive.[18]

The McElroys did eventually rejoin the production, but Lovell felt she had to maintain her guard lest her involvement in the film be diminished once again. The fact that she consented to an executive producer title continues, to this day, to obfuscate the extent to which *Picnic* was truly Lovell's passion project and production. She explains:

an argument erupted over producer credits and in my innocence I decided I would take a sole credit as executive producer while they shared producer credit ... I didn't realise that I'd practically shot myself in the foot by not having our three names as producer credit. When Hal and Jim added 'A McElroy and McElroy Production' on the selling document, I countered with 'Produced in Association with Patricia Lovell.'[19]

At this time, there were also rumours circulating within the Australian film industry that Lovell was no longer attached to the project, having been deemed too inexperienced and naïve to see it through to fruition. Regardless of this, or perhaps unaware of it,

Lovell persisted in her lonely endeavour to bring *Picnic* to the cinema screen, but encountered yet further boorish sexism from the SAFC, who insisted that an American 'screenwriter' named John Graves, who would act as their representative on the film, be co-credited alongside Lovell. They also expressed concern that Lovell held too many shares in the film's production company; she retained two shares of the vote to Weir's single vote and the McElroys' two votes, having given one to her lawyer, Maurice Isaacs, so that she would not have to face the probable situation of being outvoted on, and thereby ousted from, her *own* production. This chauvinistic attitude, quite understandably, enraged her and she remained immovable in the face of such truculent idiocy, stating later on:

how bloody dare any investor try to demean my position when they had been handed a fully developed feature film project on a plate! I was the only person who had put my own money into the long development period and held it all together.[20]

Further, Green notes in interview that there was a subsequent legal battle between himself and Graves over attribution of the screenplay, since Graves went on to work at various American universities under the entirely false pretence of having written the script for *Picnic*.[21]

It is, of course, difficult to gauge how far the passing of time has altered or shifted the cast and crew's perception of the film's making and whether some of these stories either amount to curious apocrypha or are substantially true. With regard to Lovell's story, though, I certainly discern a change in tone between interviews she took part in at the time of the film's release in 1975, and later on in 1993 when she was writing a memoir about her experiences as a woman working in the Australian film industry.[22] In the former, Lovell happily states that the McElroys were essential to *Picnic*'s making and that after two years of a disheartening struggle to negotiate with the AFDC, culminating in her amassing 11,000 AUD of personal debt over the project (more than Lovell herself made in a single year), it was only the McElroys' investment portfolio that finally convinced the AFDC to come on board with one-third of the film's production funds (a further third was supplied by the SAFC, and the rest by the film's distributor Greater Union).[23] In 1993, however, she expressed her frustration with not having her work on the film duly acknowledged by the 'three musketeers' (I presume, by this, Lovell means Weir and the McElroys), which caused an emotional rift that took time to heal. She also divulges, in this same interview, details of *Picnic*'s production and filming which needle one's conscience in light of contemporary feminist politics.[24] It was Lovell's stalwart resolve and admiration for the complexity of Lindsay's novel, as well as her impassioned faith in Weir's abilities as a visionary director, and her absolutely dogged refusal to be disregarded by a male-dominated industry (an industry which, in return, expressed negligible faith in her skill as a producer at the time), that determined *Picnic*'s sure and steady path to the cinematic screen and its consequent advent into a national canon of film-making. That her assiduous labour on *Picnic* continued (and continues) to be muddied well after the film's release – and its subsequent critical acclaim – is utterly depressing, yet all too tediously predictable. In 1995, she recalled that

Picnic had become in the industry's eyes a McElroy production and I was after all a 'new chum' in the business ... One of the film industry leaders was quoted in a magazine saying that I was 'just the girl who read the book.'[25]

I empathise with the isolating experience that Lovell sets out in retrospect in her own words and I believe – resolutely so – that without her involvement, *Picnic* (at least *this* version of it) would never have seen the light of the projection booth. *Picnic* is, unquestionably, Weir's film; yet, I contend, it also belongs indelibly to the formidable and indefatigable force that was Patricia Lovell.

Meeting with Joan Lindsay

Lovell understood that the film would never be made without the unequivocal support and endorsement of Joan Lindsay and that a personal meeting between author, director and producer would be essential, therefore, to securing the future of their project. Given the author's esoteric, near-spiritual attachment to her story, which she professed to having written in a fugue-like state over mere weeks, it was quite evident that the author herself possessed a highly singular vision of how the story should be 'imaged' or imagined; in fact, she stated in interview that the story was 'before' her eyes 'almost like

it was a film'.[26] Moreover, in casting herself as a vessel or conduit through which the story materialised itself, and by negating the line between reality and fiction in order, one assumes, to amplify the narrative's frisson of mystery, Lindsay established a dynamic by which her own psychological envisioning of the narrative's events determined the film's affective, oneiric qualities. Both Anne-Louise Lambert (Miranda St Clare) and Helen Morse (Mademoiselle de Poitiers), for instance, have spoken of Lindsay's wilful refusal to see them as artists employed in the charge of bringing her story to the screen when she came to visit the film set; instead, she chose to *see through them* to their incarnation of her own characters as if they, as actors, were not there materially right in front of her very eyes.[27] This obscuring of the boundary between dream and reality, fact and fiction, archetype and lived embodiment informs the entirety of *Picnic* as a cinematic experience; that is, as a kind of hallucination that exists liminally between states of dream and waking – or as the *dream within a dream* that the film itself conjures.

Lovell and Weir flew to Victoria and drove out to Mulberry Hill, the house in Langwarrin South which the author shared with her husband, Daryl Lindsay, the director of the National Gallery of Victoria between 1942 and 1956, and in whose office hung William Ford's oil painting from 1875, *At the Hanging Rock*. This rather prosaic fact inevitably leads to speculation that Lindsay, a consummate storyteller, overstated the quasi-hallucinatory circumstances under which the story appeared to her. Lovell's instinct about the likely connection between Weir and Lindsay proved astute, though. She said she could see 'Joan was sold on him before we left', even though Weir had contravened the advice of both Lovell and Lindsay's publisher and agent (John Taylor of F. W. Cheshire) not to ask Lindsay to explain the story's enigmatic conclusion (something which she refused to expound on and advised Weir not to ask about again, since it could only be understood as a metaphysical question).[28] Soon after the meeting, as she and Weir were about to leave Melbourne, Lovell called John Taylor on a payphone from

Tullamarine airport and offered 20,000 AUD to secure the rights
to the film, with a holding fee of 100 AUD (the entirety of Lovell's
savings at the time), which gave Lovell and Weir a grace period
of three months. It was only subsequently that Lovell and Weir
discovered that a number of people had also been trying to obtain the
rights to adaptation since 1972, all of whom Lindsay had refused.[29]
Lindsay's faith in *their* vision for the film adaptation was paramount
to her publisher agreeing to offer them the rights. This meeting had
evidently been significant for all parties concerned.

Location scouting and Hanging Rock

On the same trip, Lovell and Weir visited Mount Macedon (which
is actually a series of mountain ranges), of which the Hanging Rock
itself represents a substantial part. Mount Macedon is an inactive
or extinct volcano formed at least six million years ago that holds a
perennially sacred status for the Dja Dja Wurrung, Taungurung and
Wurundjeri Woi Wurrung people. Yet it is also a landmark around
which certain idiosyncratic forms of European and English cultural
heritage – such as horticulture and particular architectural styles –
have accrued and which mark it out further as a site of contestation
and ambivalence in relation to notions of ancient ownership and
national identity; this irresolvable tension and conflict subsists deeply

within the heart of both Lindsay's novel and Weir's film, if we choose to attend to these themes. Notably, Mount Macedon was also the chosen home of Frederick McCubbin, a painter renowned for his affiliation with the late-nineteenth-century Heidelberg school of painting, which – as we shall see – was both an avowed and profound influence on *Picnic*'s *mise en scène* and cinematography according to both Weir and Boyd.[30] It is curious, therefore, that Weir was, at the outset, indifferent to the specificity of this location and its cultural resonance within Lindsay's novel. Lovell recalls that Weir had thought that the Blue Mountain ranges would suffice as the film's location until he saw Mount Macedon in person. Lovell recollects that

[w]e suddenly drove over a rise and there on the plain below us was this eerie mass of boulders spewing out of the earth with trees emerging at strange angles from the top. Hovering over this was a single cloud. There were no other clouds in sight. It was chilling to come upon it in this way. By the time we climbed Hanging Rock and found the various natural platforms surrounded by strange boulders with animal and giant faces, we knew that no other place would do. The rock was a living character in Joan's story.[31]

Lovell, Weir, Green, Boyd and Morse have all spoken subsequently in interviews about the uncanny intensity and profound

disorientation of their embodied experiences at Hanging Rock, both prior to and during the film's shooting (the refraction of sound and light on the rock is, apparently, especially confounding in terms of one's ability to navigate direction). Morse claims that there are Aboriginal faces carved onto the Rock itself, which rendered it especially poignant for her during the scenes filmed there (the final script makes reference to this, too)[32] – although it must be said that the irony of making a film that centres on the vanishing of European white women within a country that has only lately started the process of acknowledgment and reparation for its systemic and brutal removal of Aboriginal children from their families in an attempt to 'breed out the brown' (a literal vanishing) cannot have been lost on anyone making this film. With this in mind, Weir's quizzical (perhaps even slightly churlish) comments, made in 1976, that 'Australian books tend to concentrate on the idea of being an Australian ... on the crisis of European man trying to fit into an alien environment at the bottom of the world,' and that 'these things have never interested' him 'at all' as a director, seem disingenuous (especially in light of his subsequent film, *The Last Wave*).[33] By contrast, Douglas Keesey has argued of Weir's early work (and I concur with his assessment): 'Weir's Australian films [*Picnic* and *The Last Wave*] are haunted by the uncanny in the homeland they are in the process of defining ... they are demystifications of the very myths that give white Australia its identity.'[34] Lovell herself has expressed discomfort with how the film's popularity and success directly precipitated the commodification of Hanging Rock as a tourist attraction, which she deemed (and rightly so) flagrantly insensitive to and ignorant of the Rock's sacred status for Aboriginal people. She writes:

[w]hen I revisited the Rock in 1985 it gave me the horrors and I had to leave quickly. All those old stones seemed so alive and I felt guilty for the endless stream of people clambering all over them. I seriously felt like the Rock might take retribution for what I'd done. When you're up there alone it is alive.[35]

The spiritual significance of the film's location for Australia's Aboriginal people does seem to have been of acute import to the cast and crew's collective understanding of the project on which they were all embarking – in short, that the film centres on an unavoidable anachronism that serves to foreground the absurdity of a culture that places white European settlers, a florid Italianate villa (a style that was developed in Britain at the turn of the nineteenth century) and English schoolgirls in thick, black stockings in the midst of the Australian outback. For Lovell and Green, in particular, this is the very essence of their version of *Picnic*, a film which, by extension, in and of itself represents an attempt to recuperate tropes of the Australian Gothic within the constraints of a costume drama that so evidently corrals manifold influences from European forms of 'art' cinema – and all this is done in service of (however begrudgingly) reinvigorating a national film industry. The stark ramifications of these contradictory impulses are deeply embedded in *Picnic* and reverberate disconcertingly within its viewers: the more one considers the nature of the spell that is being cast by the film (and the more one is confronted with what is only ever partially concealed from our eyes), the more its horror – its true reality, so to speak – becomes apparent.

Russell Boyd's cinematography

Imperative as it is to the film's overall effect, the spell that *Picnic* casts
so potently exceeds the unresolved mystery of its essential narrative,
then. The film has penetrated and remained within our collective
cultural imagination, I suggest, because of one of the finest and most
exacting calibrations between sound and image in cinematic history.
For this, the contributions of Russell Boyd (as cinematographer)
and Gheorghe Zamfir and Bruce Smeaton (as panpipe player and
composer respectively) remain inestimable. Image and soundtrack
dovetail to mesmerising effect in *Picnic* to conceive a markedly
peculiar and disturbing combination of discomfiting nostalgia,
poignant melancholy and unresolved terror at what remains unseen,
unknown and just out of reach. As anyone who loves the film as
much as I do can attest, *Picnic* works emotionally on the viewer
well beyond that final image of Miranda burnished for all time
into inscrutability, romantic projection and psychic loss. It retains a
formidable resonance for the viewer who becomes entranced by and
gives into its beguiling powers.

Russell Boyd has been the principal cinematographer on six
of Weir's films to date, but at the time of making *Picnic*, he had only
lensed two feature films (*Between Wars* (1974) and *The Man from
Hong Kong* (1975)) and was mostly known for his tenure at Channel
7 and Supreme Studios in Sydney – during which he made multiple
documentaries and advertisements for broadcast television. Weir
had seen Michael Thornhill's *Between Wars* and was exceptionally
impressed with Boyd's work on the film and, at the urging of Hal
McElroy (who had worked with Boyd on *Hong Kong*), approached
Boyd with a view to inviting him onto *Picnic* as cinematographer.
Although he was relatively new to the profession at the time, Boyd
seemed to understand intuitively the stylised affectation Weir would
require to envision this highly romantic world imbued with Gothic
overtones. He recalls that they had multiple conversations together
in preparation for shooting, during which they scoured the pages of
magazines and, in particular, the work of the photographer David

Hamilton (whose controversial oeuvre can, at best, be described as – if one is inclined to be generous – softly pornographic and decidedly kitsch). Boyd's background in advertising meant that he understood implicitly the specific 'special effects' that would be required to attain the 'vision' of femininity that the film constructs through an evidently male gaze. It is worth noting at this point – although I shall return to this matter at greater length – that the actress Anne Lambert, whose incarnation of Miranda is the fulcrum upon which the entirety of the film's complex priapic fantasy relies, had also worked as a model in various advertisements prior to *Picnic*. This is to say that the overtly illusory nature of *Picnic*'s representation of the female form is presented as precisely that: a deliberate and fanciful construction. Moreover, this imaginary edifice – strictly because of its very inadequacy and artificiality – both obstructs and simultaneously gestures towards the reality of the female body and female experience outside the deadening paradigm of the male gaze. This complex deployment and recuperation of manufactured images which stage a fetishistic appropriation of the female body is central to both the film's visual appeal and its disquieting undertow. As we shall see in the following chapters, Boyd's invocation of the Heidelberg school of painting (he proudly notes in interview that Tom Roberts was a distant cousin of his grandmother), his dexterous use of backlighting, reflectors, bounce light and diffusion (the entirety of *Picnic* was shot with a piece of golden-yellow wedding veil over the camera lens, after fog filters proved to be insufficient), his strategic use of telephoto lenses, his alteration of frame rate from 24 to 32 or even 50 times per second, and his deployment of still framing are cardinal to *Picnic*'s romanticised femininity presented as the direct product of a masculine, obsessive and courtly desire.[36]

As a low-budget film made on a tight shooting schedule, *Picnic* presented Boyd with multiple technical challenges, especially in terms of the scenes set on outdoor location at Hanging Rock, which were all made within a single week. The techniques used during this initial period of shooting were then adapted once the crew moved to Martindale Hall; in order to retain the luminous quality through which the girls are characterised, Boyd used mini brutes as fill light, which he filtered through spun cotton to achieve a similar effect. He also tried to tone down any effect of contrast, especially when taking close-up shots of the girls' faces, by keeping the light within two stocks of the film's exposure. This repurposing of rather standard techniques demonstrates Boyd's vivid creativity as a technician, as well as his outstanding ability to 'think' extemporaneously in light. Indeed, this was an aspect of the film's making which he relished, in part because it offered more creative freedom. Boyd states, 'one of the great things

about *Picnic* was that everything was fairly *raw* about it … the amount of equipment we had, the money we had to spend on it, the time we had to do it in … it wasn't all show at Hanging Rock'.[37] The shoot commenced on 3 February 1975 at the Rock itself (the cast and crew would then move back to Adelaide and Martindale Hall to continue shooting interior scenes, fittingly on 14 February – St Valentine's Day). In the southern hemisphere, this time of year denotes the height of the Australian summer, yet also a melancholic ripening of nature into the deeper and richer colours of autumn. The sunlight is especially bright and harsh and not at all conducive to achieving the supple and languid diffusion that defines *Picnic*'s overall aesthetic. Added to this was the intrinsic quality of the Eastman Color stock on which the film was shot, which both Boyd and Weir felt was too hard in its tone, texture and contrast. This would mean that every single shot of *Picnic* would have to be softened considerably.

Boyd worked to make the light as gentle as possible by deflection and filtration through parachute silk (in order to eliminate shadow) and diffusion through various forms of net, including the aforementioned piece of dyed wedding veil. He also tried to repurpose the natural sunlight as the major source of backlighting in order to create what he calls a 'lovely rim' around the girls' heads in close-up.[38] The overarching purpose of this was not only to soften the light, but also to minimise shadows and contrast, so as to render the girls as preternaturally smooth and luminous as if possessed of an internal glow. In order to shoot on the Rock itself, it was imperative to move several generators to both the top and midpoint of the cliff façade in order to power the multiple lights they had planned to use. However, the helicopter employed in this mission dropped one of the only two generators available, which meant that Boyd had to resort to the use of bounce light to capture the majority of these famous scenes. Boyd recalls that he used

big sheets about ten feet by ten feet, or twelve feet by twelve feet. Often it was a flat piece of polystyrene. The sort of thing you make coolers out of.

They were on metal frames. But also, I often used a hand-held piece of polystyrene, about three feet by three feet, to get in close.[39]

A further difficulty was the movement of the camera itself. Boyd resorted to use of a lightweight Arriflex because the Panavision camera – a development of the Mitchell used to shoot many films from 1930 through to 1950 – that had been allocated for use on the film's interior scenes was clearly too heavy to manipulate in such uneven and steep terrain.

These scenes required both alacrity and precise choreography on the part of Boyd and Mark Egerton (the film's first assistant director and a keen still photographer) because of the natural light conditions. They had noticed that there was a fleeting window of time during which the light was conducive to creating the effect they sought. This meant that all the scenes at the Rock had to be staged and shot in the late morning when the light was overhead the film crew and cast. Within an hour the sun moved further around, casting the landscape into the Rock's shadow once more. It was crucial that these scenes were executed with precision – a not insignificant feat when one considers that there was, at most, an hour of shooting per day over the duration of slightly more than a single week. Within this, three days alone were devoted to capturing the

lyrical panning shot of the girls at the midpoint of their ascent up the Rock. In order to achieve continuity, the lighting had to be perfect, which made for a stressful few days of filming. John Seale (the camera operator) was, according to Boyd, instrumental in designing this shot, which takes in the majesty and awe of the landscape that is about to engulf the schoolgirls.[40] It was during this week-long shoot that the striking opening images of *Picnic* were also captured. Whilst reminiscing with Weir about the challenging logistics of this initial period of shooting, Boyd recalls that

[w]e were all in the car driving to the set one morning, and as we came over the hill, we got our first view of the Rock that day. It was all shrouded in fog. It was pretty sinister. So we decided to shoot that effect right away. We flagged down the camera truck behind us and started rolling … it's not a rack-focus. It's a 'locked off' shot used twice – one with fog covering the bottom of the Rock; the other after the fog had lifted.[41]

The spellbinding opening sequence, of which these shots provide our entry point into the diegetic world, predetermines our understanding of the film as an indictment of humanity's attempts to master the natural world (a theme that recurs multiple times in *Picnic*). The Rock appears as a sovereign entity, a viewpoint from which the inhabitants of this world are observed by a force that remains indeterminate, although it is also powerfully correlated to Aboriginal presence. To remain oblivious to the natural world, the film implies, is not only an ignorant and rapacious stance to take, but parlous and even deadly for human existence.

Picnic's soundtrack and Bruce Smeaton's score

Picnic's decentring and unsettling soundtrack works on the viewer to provoke – and deliberately so – a feeling of anxiety predicated on irresolution and ambiguity. The central conceptions and tensions of *Picnic*'s narrative are embedded in the very construction of its score. Its soundtrack marries a highly unusual, yet affective world of natural sounds with classical (Bach, Mozart, Beethoven) and modern music (synthesisers, Mellotron and Romanian panpipes). Bruce Smeaton, the composer responsible for the lion's share of *Picnic*'s original score, was charged with bringing these disparate elements together and making them dovetail to subversive effect.

It was not, in fact, an affinity or correspondence between musical ideas that Weir sought, but rather to use the score as counterpoint to the image. Sonically, the film invokes the incongruity of a colonial, British notion of so-called 'civilisation' being implanted into an ancient land of which it has no comprehension. The soundtrack had to arouse a sense of something 'pagan' and 'ancient' that pre-existed and will certainly outlast everything that Appleyard College for Young Ladies and its progeny represent.[42] *Picnic* invokes the affective territory of horror by demanding that we direct our attention away from what we hear and see superficially in order to attend to what remains radically out of frame. The film foments our anxiety over what we cannot see or what remains absent within the visual field via non-diegetic sound. This aural *hors-champ*, as Saviour Catania argues, *is* the film's 'fantastic territory', for it bypasses the visual in order to effect fear psychically.[43] To put it plainly: *Picnic*'s soundtrack has to do a great deal of heavy lifting in order to disturb the film viewer. Moreover, it serves to foreshadow the film's eventual lack of resolution because of the impossible or 'desperate' (as Lovell terms it) nature of the conflict at the heart of the film's narrative and thus, necessarily, has to palpate the realm of terror. The perceptive listener will note that the genius of Smeaton's score is that its core melodic leitmotiv does not resolve but seems to loop without apparent end, whilst its uneven grouping of notes (determined by a time signature of 17/8) throws any predictable sense of rhythm off kilter. The film's soundtrack is, in other words, designed to wrong-foot us – to draw us towards something that *feels* inexorable and thus deeply troubling. Something is seemingly always slightly *off*, but we cannot articulate exactly how or why it is so. Keeping this tension in play, retaining our psychic ambivalence in relation to what is unfolding before us, was evidently paramount to Weir's vision for the film. The musical score thus became an essential component for creating what Weir has referred to as 'an [*sic*] hallucinatory, mesmeric rhythm, so that you lost awareness of facts, you stopped adding things up, and got into this enclosed atmosphere. I did everything in my power to hypnotize the audience away from the possibility of solutions'.[44] In other words, the score, in tandem with the image, works to consolidate atmosphere and ambiguity so as to foreclose a desire in the viewer for resolution. Within this, of especial note are Bach's wistful 'Prelude No. 1 in C Major' (commonly one of the first pieces children learn to play on the piano and thus perhaps inherently nostalgic), Zamfir's 'Doina: Sus Pe Culmea Dealului' and 'Doina Lui Petru Unc' (which also feature Marcel Cellier on organ), Smeaton's 'Ascent to The Rock' and a recording of an earthquake's tremors played backwards. Weir has stated his explicit intention was to draw the viewer into unease almost subliminally:

with the soundtrack I used white noise, or sounds that were inaudible to the human ear, but were constantly there on the track. I've used earthquakes a lot, for example ... I've had comments from people ... that there were odd moments during the film when they felt a strange dissociation from time and place. Those technical tricks contributed to that.[45]

2 Waiting a Million Years Just for Us: Artistic Influences and Uncanny Spaces

As I said at the opening of this book, *Picnic* is a film of psychological terror that takes place in daylight. I now want to examine the quality of that light, but I also want to attend to its recesses of shadow and shade. To what is this light blinding us? What is it that we fear might dwell in the shadows? Why is this diegetic world at once so familiar and yet so arcane? Why does this vision leave us with such a tremulous and aching sense of unease that cannot be readily or merely attributed to the film's lack of solution? *Picnic* draws on a rich artistic inheritance of a coterie of nineteenth-century Australian painters who were heavily indebted in terms of influence to the European Impressionist tradition. If we are to attempt to answer these questions, it is incumbent on us to understand the ways in which *Picnic* recuperates this (actually rather short-lived) artistic tradition in order to destabilise the security and insistence of specific notions of nationalism and homeland for which the Heidelberg School's oeuvre – and that of Australian Impressionism broadly – stood.[46]

The Heidelberg School

Pivotal to the establishment of what has come to be known as the Heidelberg School (named after the suburban town north-east of Melbourne in which many of the school's associated artists gathered to paint) was the *9 by 5 Impression Exhibition*. This selection of 183 paintings by, most notably, Tom Roberts (perhaps the most celebrated artist of this group), Charles Condor and Arthur Streeton, was exhibited in August 1889 in downtown Melbourne and took its name from the dimensions of the wooden cigar boxes on which the artists had rendered their scenes of recognisably Australian landscapes, burgeoning industrial cities (such as Melbourne and Sydney) and naval ports. Roberts and Streeton in particular had lately returned from Europe where they had sought to establish themselves as artists. Exposed to the latest techniques in *plein-air* painting and even undertaking further training – in Roberts's case – at the Royal Academy (where Streeton would go on to exhibit in 1900), they travelled between major European cities and absorbed the wealth of artistic collections that galleries and museums had to offer. For Streeton in particular, this residency in London, which he regarded as the home of the British Empire, instilled a fervent sense of patriotism towards the colonial project – a notion that, alongside exciting artistic developments, he exported home to Australia and translated into his paintings. The *9 to 5 Impression Exhibition* coincided with a tumescent movement towards strategic political alliance and unification within Australia. The year 1888 marked the centenary of British settlement and by 1901 the federation of Australia pronounced, for the white European population of Australia, the establishment of their nation, as they would come to think of it. Of cardinal importance to Australian Impressionism, then, was the specificity of a newly formed sense of national identity that should be reflected in and refracted through a definitively Australian style of painting.

As such, painting outdoors using techniques designed to capture the momentary 'impressions' of an ephemeral and kaleidoscopic natural landscape became an endeavour of seemingly national importance as Australia sought to inaugurate its own identity as distinct from specifically British traditions and Victorian values. As a result, certain ideals and attributes (strength, fortitude, intrepid exploration) that were felt keenly to be intrinsic to modern Australian national identity also accrued to this style of impressionist painting. Whilst the quintessential landscapes such as the rural suburbs of Melbourne and the white sandy beaches of Sydney regularly featured, the specific creation of a myth of national identity was promulgated by cleaving an image of the heroic white settler (typically embodied in the farmer figure) to the land which he seeks to bring under control and tame into order. These strikingly beautiful images that pertain to tropes of naturalism obscure both the reality of the colonial project (that this 'homeland' is in no sense the 'home' of white settlers and that the land itself was never ceded) and the brutal decimation of ancient Indigenous cultures. As I sit here writing this book in 2021, during a period in history that is not only post-Mabo but has also ushered in a cultural and political reckoning with the physical and psychic damage of legacies of coloniality still bodied forth within people and writ large across land, it would be flagrantly negligent not to acknowledge the violence that these light-filled and exquisite portraits work so assiduously to conceal – a violence endemic, one might add, to the very project of empire.[47]

It is perhaps ironic that in seeking to establish a modern Australian identity in keeping with the transition towards federation, an art form that would come to be tied intrinsically to a 'national' style of painting would invoke an artistic legacy such as Impressionism that is so indelibly married to white European culture. In tying this form to an Australian milieu, these images could not (and cannot) help but assert colonialism as the very essence of the identity that they were (and arguably still are) seeking to shore up: that is, the transposition of European (and especially British) values and cultural identity to the Australian landscape and the white population. By turning away from English colonial styles of painting that took a quasi-anthropological approach (which in and of itself was often suspect) to depicting Indigenous people within the archetypal topography of Australian bushland and desert, these painters sought to replace Aboriginal presence with that of the white settler. To ally a body to a landscape is never a neutral gesture and this artistic project served an expedient political purpose in attempting to naturalise the presence of a fundamentally European population within Aboriginal land.

Picnic's recuperation of Australian Impressionism: anatomy of a sequence

Picnic's visual appeal is partially predicated on this artistic heritage (which serves as a constant – yet troubled and convoluted – backdrop), whilst the film, in turn, knowingly draws on European styles of 'arthouse' cinema in order to establish a unique form of Australian cinema. This alliance, though, is an uneasy one. Whereas Australian Impressionism as an artistic form was indubitably marked by a fierce resolve to establish a new kind of Australian identity as the country turned towards a future it sought to determine for itself beyond Victorian values and society, the film itself is insistently disturbed by its curious fusion of nostalgia with foreboding. On one level, Picnic very apparently circulates around a void of meaning, an absence of explanation; but on a more subsistent level – which is harder to articulate – its fine calibration of beauty with portentous shadow, the manner in which it offsets the carefree excitement of female adolescence with both a melancholic presentiment of loss and an initially vague and then insistent apprehension of harm, presages something far more overtly disturbing than the artistic legacy to which it owes a debt. I contend that what unsettles us in Picnic is something deeply rooted in the very construction of whiteness and white identity within a land that, contrary to the halcyon and bucolic patriotic portraiture of the nineteenth century, remains, by definition, vast and unknowable to a people who cannot hope to understand it, let alone control and fashion it in their own image. Picnic's seeming nostalgia for the period of its setting – which it so lovingly recreates – is, in effect, imbued with Gothic sensibilities and unavoidably tainted by the uncanny. The visual pleasure Picnic affords us as viewers is far from simple, artless indulgence. Indeed, its panoply of artistic reference points, even beyond the Heidelberg School, is composite and altogether strange.

The scene of the picnic itself is exceptionally rich visually. Every frame of these two sequences (divided by a cross-cut back to Mrs Appleyard and Sara Waybourne in the college) matches the aesthetic

qualities of the Australian Impressionist movement. Yet whilst the palate of the Heidelberg School evidently informs every shot in these scenes, there are two further images that are directly invoked: William Ford's aforementioned *At the Hanging Rock* (1875), and Sandro Botticelli's *The Birth of Venus* (1485). Sustained analysis reveals intricate facets of framing, lighting, sound and editing that serve to undercut any facile recuperation or recycling of these diverse reference points. As Mr Hussey's wagon draws close to the Rock, the first thing that is immediately apparent to the viewer is the contrast between the burnished greens and browns of the bushland and the pristine, reflective whiteness of the girls' dresses. Visually, the chromatic scale seems to allude to images such as Frederick McCubbin's *Lost* (1886), in which the presence of a lost child (Clara Crosbie, a young girl who went missing in the bush for three weeks) within the vast and engulfing expanse of nature is marked out by her white apron and straw hat. This correlation is rendered even more apparent by a later panning shot that tracks the movement of the girls (Miranda, Irma, Marion and Edith) through the undergrowth as they hurry towards the Rock. In this shot, their quicksilver movement is partially obscured by long grass, trees and foliage, and it is specifically the stark luminosity of their feminine attire that differentiates them from their environment. *Lost* is an especially curious image within the canon of Australian Impressionism because it captures the rugged beauty of the bush, but also evokes a terrifying undercurrent of what it might be like to be swallowed up by the natural world. It is, in fact, far closer to the thematic territory of the Sublime than other paintings within this genre and is thus an entirely apposite point of reference for *Picnic*.

It is significant that it is Miranda who unlatches the gate between the gentrified path and the site of Hanging Rock in this first plane of action. Although she is only on screen for less than a third of the film's running time, Miranda functions as a conduit or vessel in the minds of both the diegetic characters and the viewers – this is even apparent in the way that her dialogue seems to be delivered *through* her and not *by* her. Her action here unleashes a

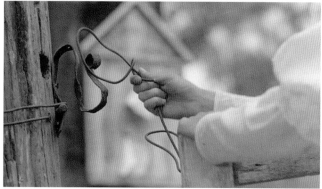

series of superimpositions that portend forces beyond human sight
or control: a flock of birds consume the screen, their movement
erasing continuity of direction; the carriage horses rear up and bray
at something that remains obscure to the human eye; and the airy, yet
precise melodic refrain of Zamfir's panpipes reminds us that we are
in the territory of something 'pagan' and 'ancient'. A single dissolve
moves the picnic party to the foot of the Rock. Captured in a low-
angle framing, which here is suggestive of a specular force that bears
down on them from on high, it is once again Miranda who carries
the action forward. In honour of Saint Valentine, she cuts into a large

and florid, heart-shaped cake that, in close-up, is rendered vaguely grotesque. The soundtrack resonates with the rhythmic timbre of a slow earthquake, suggesting further that some kind of inexorable force has been set in motion.

The second scene set at the foot of the Rock opens with a close-up of Miranda, framed under a rosy-pink sun parasol and limned by sunlight. Her left eye is enlarged by a magnifying glass, through which she is examining a delicate yellow flower. This shot positions Miranda as a seer, an agent of knowledge – and indeed, she functions as a tabula rasa onto whom the other characters project knowledge (later on Sara will claim that Miranda knows things that other people do not). Yet it is also striking that she is studying a flower, since Miranda herself is frequently aligned with images of nature coming into bloom; clearly, this is a somewhat generic way of alluding to her being on the threshold of womanhood, but it also signifies some essential way in which she is not seen for who she really is, as a girl. This image, in contradistinction to prior and ensuing images of Miranda which compound her specularity or *to-be-looked-at-ness*, could be viewed as her own desire for self-knowledge: that is, to understand the constraints of femininity (a set of qualities which Appleyard College

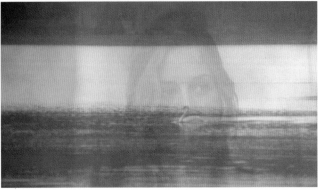

for Young Ladies cultivates in preparation for a life lived within further patriarchal institutions).[48] Later, of course, Miranda's image will be scrutinised under the magnifying glass of Colonel Fitzhubert and distorted into a swan by the imagination of his nephew, Michael.

A fluid panning shot from screen right to left unfolds a form of cinematic still life. This sequence and the long shot proceeding it seem to be a direct allusion to Ford's *At the Hanging Rock*: both images are precisely composed to frame the human figure as diminutive within the natural landscape; both images convey bodies picked out within the frame via shadow and light; and both images centrally frame a plane of action within a shaft of sunlight. What the film image does, of course, is to draw this still life into movement. Yet the pace of movement is notably languorous and the central protagonists (somnambulists) either recline or sit whilst the natural and insect worlds remain in perpetual, busy motion all around them (to which they seem oblivious). Overlaying this shot, we hear one of the girls recite Shakespeare's famous Sonnet 18 ('Shall I compare thee to a summer's day?'). The invocation of this specific meditation on youthful beauty further complicates the unfolding action, for if Shakespeare finds nature wanting – inconstant and insubstantial – and thus inadequate as metaphor for his beloved's grace, here it is nature which is the perennial constant that will outlast the vagaries of fleeting youth.

For in *Picnic*, the ripening of female youthfulness is inextricably bound up with loss and death. Tellingly, Miranda's delicate silver belt buckle is a butterfly, which might designate a life destined for brevity (or preservation as a prized commodity or collector's item). The flower that she holds in her hand has been plucked from the earth that sustains it – its beauty is transitory and destined to diminish and wilt. The flowers that the girls pick and preserve in a press provide an apt metaphor not only for their own condition (the restraints and suffocation of Victorian ideals of femininity), but also for the psychological mechanisms the film itself invokes. If for Shakespeare it is, finally, the security of his iambic pentameter that will preserve the beloved for eternity, the film similarly seems to yoke the aestheticised likeness of these young women into cinematic history and the minds of viewers. In other words, *Picnic*'s affectively melancholic register works through an already embodied knowledge of what is irreparably lost to time: that the past is fundamentally irretrievable, that nostalgia is a painful, futile and often dangerous force, and that there is no deliverance from death.

It is precisely at this moment that Mr Hussey notes that his watch has stopped 'dead' on '12 o'clock' – something which the cerebral Greta McCraw attributes to magnetic forces (whereas we might invoke cinematic dead time). The exactitude of timing in *Picnic* – the year 1900, 14 February, 12 o'clock – bears further scrutiny. The characters are – unbeknownst to them – caught up in a world that is in transition politically and culturally. Portrayed, in effect, through a still-life tableau (iterated in the subsequent cut to a long shot which provides the graphic match to Ford's painting), the film itself suggests that these are characters who represent an old guard, a vehemently Victorian society whose long-reigning monarch stands in for a sense of security gleaned from utter intransigence to change. This stasis, this sense of entitled arrogance – expressed openly by schoolgirl Edith, who believes that they are 'the only living creatures in the whole world' – is directly belied by the environment surrounding them, which is teeming with movement and life. In close-up, a dissection of the Valentine's

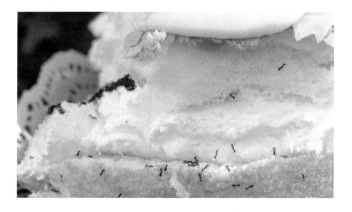

Day cake appears as a geological edifice replete with grotesque strata, all of which is being busily consumed by an industrious army of ants. Moreover, the year, the season and the hour mark out inherently liminal moments portending incontrovertible alteration (as a rite of passage): the transition away from Victorian Britain, the autumnal shift into a season marked by a loss of light, hibernation and death, and an hour that marks the slow bleed from morning into afternoon, and evening into night. Well before Miranda (the film's eternal source of light and knowledge) disappears, we know that what this graphic match denotes is the undeniable end of an era that has prided and comforted itself falsely on absolute moral certainty and entitlement.

As Miranda tells Mlle de Poitiers that they will only 'be gone a little while', we might recall Greta McCraw's recent statement to the girls that one million years is a relatively short period of time geologically speaking (in fact Hanging Rock is, of course, far older). Various scholars have delineated time as experienced by the characters at the Rock through the concept of Aboriginal Dreamtime.[49] It seems to me that such an allusion can only ever be made in a hopelessly clumsy fashion by those (and I count myself amongst their number) who are not intimately acquainted with Aboriginal life and its knowledge. As Stephanie Gauper points out, even thinking of this concept in terms of time is a misnomer, since

the Aborigines define being in terms of place and space rather than time. For them time does not precede event; events simply occur and there are no ultimate precedents, origins. Time beginning and ending are impossible concepts for them to entertain. Dreaming is not a time but a symbol, a location and a source of energy.[50]

It is quite clear that Weir, taking his cue from Lindsay, tried to incorporate such ideas somewhat nebulously into the dialogue delivered by Miranda, Irma and Marion whilst on the Rock, shortly before their disappearance. However, I believe that these seemingly 'mystical' musings issued through the girls are better explained as an attempt to intimate the themes explored in Lindsay's infamous redacted final chapter, which she had tried to repurpose within the book's third chapter to uneven effect. What *is* apparent is that this line is meant to be prophetic of, in particular, Miranda's mysterious disappearance and her subsequent reinscription within memory. For it is precisely *this* moment in the film in which she is transformed into one of cinema's most defining iconic images of youthful female beauty. The melody carried by the panpipes does, of course, help to cast this highly peculiar cinematic spell, but it is the transition from mid-shot (as Mlle de Poitiers's point of view) to close-up (a position technically impossible for any of the characters) that renders Miranda as icon. Here, she is captured as an ideational representation in both the mind of Poitiers *and* that of the viewer; that the film will conclude on this image, which has been pulled into stillness by an increased frame rate and finally fades out, is significant. As such, the film imitates the way in which loss, especially of a loved one, is incorporated into memory as a moment out of time. This capture, psychologically, signals an attempt to wrest life from 'time's relentless melt', but also to cover over the void left in the wake of death with a cherished (and fetishised) image that can never make good the lack.[51] This kind of image is one created as a form of talisman against death as ultimate, unknowable and meaningless void ('nothing to love or link with').[52]

It is Mlle de Poitiers who, in this moment, defines how Miranda is to be seen posthumously: as a 'Botticelli angel'. This is a curious description because the image she is likening Miranda to is in fact *The Birth of Venus*. This hybrid characterisation of Miranda as both goddess and celestial being is cardinal to understanding the film's ideological construction of femininity as both other-worldly and yet as natural as a pearl (although notably, the formation of a pearl is dependent on intrusion and interference), as both sexual and virginal, as both physical presence and absent object of desire. Miranda is made to bear the burden of multiple forms of feminine iconicity here. And just as Botticelli's Venus, rendered in pearlescent tempura and gold gilding, is designed to emanate light, Miranda too is sutured into our collective memory as a preternaturally lovely creature in diaphanous white muslin outlined by sunlight. She is *designed* to be unforgettable. Miranda St Clare (the film need not, in fact, divulge her surname, for it is embedded in her very form) is here transformed into a divine intermediary between this life and beyond, between earth and the heavens (if this is what we choose to believe). In effect, her ghost precedes her: her embodied reality is transformed into *the* image that will continue to return and to haunt. As such, she figures doubly and is potentially disrupting for it. And yet we also know that this is an elaborate fantasy invoked to cope with traumatic loss and, most tellingly, to avoid the violent reality of what might really have happened to four young girls who go missing in treacherous terrain – only two of whom return physically safe ('intact'), yet psychologically scarred for all time.

National identity and the return of the repressed

Picnic readily draws upon an intimate connection between notions of the uncanny (as a return of what has been repressed) and broader definitions of the Gothic applicable to national (and geographical) narratives. Sigmund Freud was certainly not the first person to elaborate the uncanny as a theoretical concept (Freud takes his cue from Ernst Jentsch's paper on the topic from 1906), but his development has been the most widely appropriated and used within the field of aesthetics (perhaps because of Freud's own evident interest in its literary forms). Freud delineates the specificity of the uncanny (*das Unheimlich*) by contrasting it to what appears to be superficially 'homely' (*das Heimlich*) – as a designation of everything to which we are already accustomed. He writes that

we are reminded that the word 'heimlich' is not unambiguous, but belongs to two sets of ideas, which, without being contradictory, are yet very different: on the one hand it means what is familiar or agreeable, and on the other, what is concealed and kept out of sight. 'Unheimlich' is customarily used … [as] the contrary of the first signification … and not of the second.[53]

Crucially, Freud extends Friedrich Wilhelm Schelling's thesis on the uncanny in order to emphasise that *das Unheimlich* correlates to that which 'ought to have remained secret and hidden but has come to light'; by extension, he asserts that *das Heimlich* can only ever *seemingly* denote a space that is 'free of ghostly influences', since its very definition 'develops in the direction of ambivalence until it finally coincides with its opposite'.[54] If we are able to characterise the uncanny as that which relates properly to a class of things that is truly frightening and, thus, which is capable of arousing terror in the observer, Freud complicates this further by stating that if

psycho-analytic theory is correct in maintaining that every affect belonging to an emotional impulse ... is transformed, if it is repressed, into anxiety, then among instances of frightening things there must be one class in which the frightening element can be shown to be something repressed which *recurs* ... if this is indeed the secret nature of the uncanny, we can understand why linguistic usage has extended *das Heimlich* into its opposite; for this uncanny is in reality nothing new or alien, but has become something which is familiar and old-established in the mind and which has become alienated from it only through the process of repression.[55]

It is the *return* of what has been repressed, the unveiling or revelation of that which *should have been kept hidden* from view in order to shore up what is homely and familiar that is imperative to Freud's definition of the uncanny. Fundamentally then, to lay claim to one's home – as land – may be a comforting narrative trope, but it is forged through potent forces of repression. Further, the disturbance or disruption of that narrative, which in the case of *Picnic* corrals the white settler's assumption of inalienable rights and supposedly sovereign identity as the bearer of 'civilisation', effects a crack or fissure through which alternate histories and narratives can enter.

Film, as a technology of mediation, is able to play on our atavistic anxieties by troubling our sense of reality. A variety of cinematic devices are employed in helping to achieve and maintain an effect of reality on screen – everyone knows that it would be jejune in the extreme to assume that even documentary images accord with an unassailable notion of truth. Cinema foments its most destabilising and upsetting *affects* on viewers through the collision between that which seems to conform to what is familiar and assuring, and that which flagrantly overturns or decentres our most basic assumptions about the world and our place within it. Central to this is its ability to play on that which is excluded from the frame of vision. Stephen Heath suggests that this is, in fact, the very condition of cinema, of visibility, itself. In effect, cinema, for Heath (extending Jacques Lacan's *Seminar XI: The Four Fundamental Concepts of Psychoanalysis*), is tantamount to that which 'remains over as the point from which the frame is framed, the troubling blind spot in vision from where the images look back'.[56]

Picnic, as Alison Horbury argues, draws on this 'troubling blind spot' to effect a 'disturbance' in 'the national Imaginary'.[57] She contends:

[s]tructurally, the Rock becomes a vanishing point in the film where, though perceptible in the visual field, it is shot from a low angle such that its crevices appear anthropomorphically as a (possibly Indigenous) face that looks back at the viewer, disturbing the viewing position as one of controlling mastery or 'all seeing'.[58]

It is intriguing that cast, crew, scholars and viewers alike tend to regard this gaze that 'looks back' as an Aboriginal presence that un-masters the white colonial fantasy of settled space as homeland; for as Michael Bliss has noted: 'what *Picnic* cites without actually including ... are the dark "others" ... their presence in *Picnic*, which is exaggeratedly Caucasian in conception, is made manifest both by their virtual invisibility in the film ... and their association with the rock'.[59]

Picnic is structured around this conspicuous absence of Aboriginal life; in fact, in problematically rendering Aboriginal

presence as a spectral absence, it also works to construct what
Elspeth Tilley has called a 'fearful space', in which the failure to see,
to master and to control is also allied with the emergence of 'illusions,
irrationality ... [and] the supernatural'. It is also striking that within
fearful space, it is white people who are terrorised, victimised and
subject to inexplicable disappearance.[60] In essence, the outback is
recuperated as a parlous and threatening space that at once shores
up the bravery and courage of white settler narratives, but also
casts Aboriginal life as symbolically (and menacingly) 'other' – a
structuring device that is always kept at bay through Victorian
rigmarole and ritual to the point of redundancy and exhaustion in
Picnic. In cleaving horror to the natural landscape, which in its sheer
vastness is perceived as hostile and minacious, *Picnic* is exemplary
of the Australian Gothic aesthetic in which repressed and seemingly
sinister forces return to disrupt the present.[61]

What is revealed in the return is, on the one hand, the very
force of a cultural repression effected on a grand scale by which
the sovereignty of Aboriginal life is denied; on the other hand, it
also renders apparent the unconscious fears of the white settler
and the fierce potency of psychic mechanisms, such as projection
and transference. For it is the white imaginary that determines the
unsettled space as dangerously 'other', as a perverse form of container

for all the violent impulses and drives which it is so absolutely adamant to deny within itself. In interview, Weir has stated that

[w]e, forty million of us, live hard along the coasts. We're mostly in the cities on the edge of this vast continent. It's just there to be seen if you live there. It affects you even if you're not conscious of it – that great emptiness.[62]

What Weir evocatively describes as an 'emptiness' here is one of the oldest living cultures on Earth – a culture that is insistently present despite determined efforts to deracinate and decimate it. That Indigenous life is experienced and delineated as a 'void' within white colonial culture is indeed indicative of substantial psychic repression, but it also evinces a sustained and very-much-conscious attempt to render Indigeneity spectral and absent in order to declare Indigenous land as *terra nullius*. Douglas Keesey has outlined this as Australia's reckoning with its 'national uncanny', a process through which all that has been repressed from the 'master' narrative of 'civilisation' returns as a force of interruption and disturbance. Keesey states, 'the bush reminds white Australians of the vast extent to which they are not at home in their homeland, that their national identity is founded on repression of all that must be kept "outback"'.[63] The hubris endemic to the white colonial imaginary and its project – its desire to render all that it surveys in the image of itself, and its ultimately futile impulse to control and order – is radically exposed in this return. For this 'threat', which induces in us such outsized fear, that seems to impinge on us from elsewhere – from outside – *is* a psychic projection: it is terrifying not because the violence lies in wait for us 'out there' in the 'darkness', but because it is born and dwells within our own small hearts and minds.

Ascent to the Rock: anatomy of a sequence

The girls' slow and steady ascent to the peak of Hanging Rock is one of the most celebrated sequences within Australia's cinematic heritage. Cinematography, lighting, editing, sound and acting style dovetail here to truly compelling effect and thus, unsurprisingly, it is often these moments that viewers recall long after their first encounter with *Picnic*. Attentive close reading of this sequence unearths an intricate structure that works through motifs such as repetition, mirroring and de-framing to figure precisely a seemingly absent presence that *looks back* at us. The sequence progresses through four stages of action which increasingly destabilise the viewer's relationship to space, time and causality, thus implying that it is the Rock itself which determines the mysterious events that stand in for the void of meaning around which *Picnic* circulates.

In the first plane of action, we join the scene *in media res* as if the entry of Smeaton's plaintive and unremitting piano refrain has transported the girls straight from the relative safety of the picnic party and its surroundings to the perilous rock face; the framing of this initial sequence is imperative to the relentless accretion of unease that we will feel as events unfold. Panning downwards from an expanse of open sky to the Rock's edifice, the camera tracks to screen left and frames the girls coming into view; although held centrally in the frame, they are obscured and partially concealed by tall and dry bush grass and reframed in a trajectory that tracks from screen right to left. Of importance here is that the camera has seemingly anticipated their movement and that their journey is cast in reverse (as a return). As we shall see, there are several violations of screen direction that work to confound the viewer's ability to map the diegetic space together. A cut to a low-angle profile shot of Miranda, possibly rendered through a telephoto lens, serves to flatten her visually against the textured rock face that appears to tower over her diminutive frame. What we can assume to be Miranda's point of view (a position the film mostly refuses to afford us) reveals the monumental size of the Rock that bears down on her. The profile shot of Miranda is subsequently graphically matched with Irma, Marion and Edith all held in profile, as if to suggest that nature is equally indifferent to the four lives trespassing through it and will exert a powerful force over each of them, whether they are destined to disappear into oblivion or to survive. As the musical

refrain swells with the additional timbre of the Mellotron, the visual track cuts to two highly unusual vantage points: first, from an angle positioned directly above and yet within relative proximity to the girls – and thus more suggestive of the Rock itself as the source of the gaze, rather than any nebulous 'eye of God'; and second, from a contrasting extreme low angle that positions the Rock as an anthropomorphised presence looking down on us directly (thus we are refused identification with the mastery presupposed in the former shot). Further, the speed with which the clouds drift in this second shot suggests a canted perception of time's passing. We may note additionally that the clouds' trajectory contradicts that of the girls, so that visually we have the impression of shifting planes of movement – the contrapuntal force of the natural world set against human desire and best-laid plans – which is, in turn, also felt formally through the uneven grouping of notes within the musical score itself. As I mentioned previously, this cinematic world is calibrated to play on our anxieties by seeming at once both familiar and yet radically strange. Something is *off*, even if we cannot articulate how it is so.

A subsequent cut to mobile mid-shot positions the girls' movement now from screen left to right (the camera has crossed the axis of action); here, once again, the stark whiteness of their diaphanous dress contrasts with the chromatic tones of yellowish-green and brown. This cut to action initiates the renowned circular panning shot from screen right to left (once again, we have contrapuntal movement within the frame). We can observe that the girls have now reached the midpoint of their ascent and they are engulfed by dense foliage. As the camera completes its 360-degree rotation, it reframes the girls ascending ever higher towards the Rock's peak, as if in tandem with the insistent and rising change of key within the score. The overall effect is one of enclosure, both within the natural environment and the cinematic frame, as if their ultimate disappearance – if we read this to be unwilled

or unmotivated – will be the result of undisclosed forces beyond their charge or comprehension. They are caught within the frame of an alternate plane of motion that is only vaguely intuited. The subsequent cut repositions this vantage point from *within* the Rock from a location that seems, once again, to divine the girls' movements. This effects a seemingly unidentified point of view onto the action which observes their presence. We notice subsequently that Miranda, Irma and Marion have formed a chain, whilst Edith has broken away and remains trailing behind the trio. Edith's gaze has remained resolutely focused on the path immediately under her feet, much to Miranda's consternation, suggesting that she is far more concerned with mapping and marking out her itinerary (possibly leaving a trail in the dust and soil) than the other girls, who appear to be pulled involuntarily, like somnambulists or automata, towards the Rock.

As the piano refrain fades, there is a perceptible shift in tone from melodramatic Gothicism (young ladies in imminent peril) to a far more troubling, elusive and abstract sense of harm that now seems to pervade the diegesis. I contend that this is the second stage of the girls' ascent. The inverted, uncanny sounds of an earthquake, though non-diegetic, seem to emanate directly from the Rock itself. We return to an overhead framing that traces the girls as they move between the Rock's crevices, their ambulation recalling that of the

ants to whom nobody paid much mind or notice. This shot, once
again, is juxtaposed with several equally oblique angles from inside
the Rock, which work together to reframe the girls within a hermetic
and claustrophobic space that is also suggestive, once more, of an
anonymous point of view. Of immediate note is the markedly slower
frame rate precipitated by Miranda moving into view from behind the
other girls, which is offset by the subsequent low-angled mid-shot of
the Rock's face looming down from under a sea of fast-rolling cloud.
Time is, certainly, 'out of joint'. A cut to a strikingly tight framing of
the back of Miranda's head moves us into the ambivalent position
of either being in the same space as the girls or being an indefinite
presence that stalks their movement. This effect is formally known as
décadrage, a term originally elaborated on by theorist Pascal Bonitzer
as a style of framing that serves to heighten apprehension by playing
on what remains just out of sight at the periphery of the film frame;
here, the human body in particular is rendered vulnerable through
techniques that serve either to engulf it in a vast space or enclose it
within a tight and extremely close frame (both of which are employed
in *Picnic*). Cardinal to this uncanny and disturbing effect is the
seemingly unmotivated position from which we see the action taking
place. This sense of impending threat or harm is often necessarily
attributed to that which lies outside of our immediate frame of
reference and thus it draws on our fear of the unknown (what we do
not see and hear – or what we hear, but do not see).[64]

It may seem that this reading is overdetermined, but attentive
deconstruction of the scene reveals something very strange. Miranda's
physical location shifts several times: initially, the other three girls
pass in front of her so that she becomes the final girl to bring up the
line; so when Miranda turns around and speaks directly towards the
location from which the camera takes up perspective and says softly,
'We can't go much further. We promised Mademoiselle we wouldn't
be long away', it has the effect of disorientating us because it seems it
cannot be one of the other girls to whom she is talking. Momentarily,
it seems as if she is speaking to *the viewer*, who is placed within the

disquieting position of identifying with a gaze that seems to emanate from an unknown source. It is only the subsequent shot that can be read as *retroactively* justifying the former anonymous perspective, since we discern that there has been a curious time lapse by which Miranda has shifted place once again from last girl to first girl. That this transformation is also latterly inferred through that brief cross-cut back to a low angle of the Rock's 'face' in profile offset against a rolling cloud formation now moving in the opposite direction to its previous pattern (and which divides the girls' progression through the rocky crevice) is also significant. Coupled with the effect of increased frame rate, the viewer is gradually coaxed into attributing agency to the Rock as an anthropomorphised presence that is shifting not only the girls' relationship to space and time, but also that of the viewer. In short, this brief sequence works to disrupt our relationship to time, causality and spatial orientation, only then to reassure and placate us – yet we cannot rid ourselves of the sense that something is being powerfully shifted around with regards to the relationship between perception and knowledge. It seems significant that Miranda utters 'we wouldn't be long away' as if it were some form of incantation issued or given voice through her, a pronouncement that seems to usher in (via another strategic cut) the musical motif carried by the panpipes (which, we recall, were chosen to invoke 'the old gods').

As she approaches the mouth of the crevice, she appears to be merging with the light. We have moved to a higher plane of action (literally and metaphorically): the third stage of the ascent.

Despite Edith's efforts to tether the ongoing events to earthier matters by discussing Sara's proclivity for writing love poems to Miranda whilst ensconced in the lavatory (perhaps suitably rendered in conventional shot and reverse shot), this sequence is marked by a series of overlapping dissolves which work to raise the tone towards the metaphysical. Miranda reminds Edith that Sara is an orphan and Irma likens her to an injured deer whom she rescued but was 'doomed to die'. She recites the first few lines of Felicia Hemans's 'Casabianca': 'The boy stood on the burning deck, whence all but he had fled.' This is curious not only because the lines intimate how duty, loyalty and servitude can blind us to imminent danger (and as such, we can infer that Sara is not the only being within this vehemently colonial world who is 'doomed'), but also provokes us into questioning Mrs Appleyard's obscure origins. We recall here that cross-cut into the scenes set at the foot of the Rock are those back at the college where Appleyard is trying to enforce on the orphaned Sara the distinctly dubious pleasure of committing 'The Wreck of the Hesperus' to memory. That Appleyard summarily dismisses Sara's own attempts at poetry in favour of that of 'Mrs Hemans' is telling, for she has misattributed the poem (Henry Wadsworth Longfellow is its author). As such, Appleyard is a purveyor of falsehoods (this single instance forces us to question the entirety of her narrative), a fact that she evidently tries to cover over with pomposity and a hectoring manner – it is no wonder that she finally turns to drink and incontinent bouts of nostalgia when the edifice of her self-deception starts to crumble. It is Irma who invokes Hemans's words appropriately – almost eerily so – on the Rock (regardless of the fact that she cannot recall beyond a portion of the opening stanza). As such, we are led to believe that these girls possess a knowledge already quite beyond Appleyard's deceitful, cruel mind and everything her establishment represents. Indeed, what transpires situates them (with the exception of Edith, whose thoughts remain resolutely focused on more 'schoolgirlish' matters) as visionaries.

The sequence of dissolves effects a direct relationship between Miranda and Irma: two young women destined to have very different fates on the Rock. Whereas Miranda, having been recast as a totemic sacrifice to some arcane higher power, becomes the container for male phantasy and courtly desire precisely *because* of her absence, Irma returns as the repository of a dangerous and possibly carnal knowledge that threatens to rupture the 'genteel' carapace of civility so rigidly set in place at Appleyard College – a screen that obscures the wanton sadism and violence that fashions young girls into 'ladies'. Visually, these shots work to render the female body immanent within the enclaves and texture of the Rock itself and contribute towards a well-trammelled (and problematic) allegiance between femininity and nature that is powerfully constitutive of *Picnic*'s visual appeal.

This series of ten shots is initiated by a close-up of the back of Miranda's head as she pivots to face the viewer; instead of bringing the background plane into focus by racking, a superimposition of the rock face adumbrated by the light of sunset moves across the screen from left to right and across Miranda's face, which remains framed in close-up; this shot resolves into a mid-shot of the rock face, which images the path in between the crevice towards which the girls will be drawn, and binds Miranda to Irma via dissolve. As such, it is now the Rock which seems to connect the fate of these two young lives (and not merely Appleyard College). As the image resolves into a mid-shot of Irma standing astride one of the Rock's outer-lying peaks, we observe that she has removed both her laced boots and opaque black stockings (those hallmarks of Victorian feminine propriety); Irma sways gently from side to side, lifting the skirts of her dress, her body set against an open expanse of bushland that stretches out beyond the Rock. A further dissolve moves the sequence back to a close-up of Miranda, who is this time seen in profile and turns to look upwards and out of frame; this resolves into a low-angle frame of Irma on the Rock who, since the sunlight is behind her, appears to be shot

through with light as she continues her slow dance. The rhythmic calibration of the images now established, we dissolve back into a shot of Miranda removing her stockings and resolve back to Irma, who is now held in close-up at a low angle and at an increased frame rate. The subsequent dissolve to a superimposition of Irma dancing onto a shot of Miranda and Marion's bare feet on the rock face is notable because Irma figures doubly here. As such, Irma is seen to be dancing with her own shadow, thus presaging the fundamental way in which her life will be ruptured, that she will be split between the way of life to which she returns (although incontrovertibly changed) and her 'shadow' self whom she leaves behind on the Rock. We can also regard this as a direct allusion to Lindsay's interest in quantum time travel. The gentle rhythmic pace of these images that oscillate between dissolution and resolution, reality and dream, lulls the viewer into a hypnotic state. The delicate and airy quality of Zamfir's panpipes also evokes ambiguity and irresolution. The girls have entered a liminal state in which they seem to function increasingly like passengers between this world and an undefined space that is perceived only obliquely through atmospheric qualities. It is solely Edith – who remains resolutely herself and, as such, is aghast at what she deems to be her classmates' state of disarray ('where in the world are they going? *without their shoes!*') – who will return from

this moment. The other three girls will henceforth act like conduits or vessels in their speech, whilst their movements will take on a perceptibly somnambulist or automaton-like quality (an intrinsic feature of Freud's delineation of the uncanny). It is, indeed, as if they are undertaking a rite of passage that is moving towards its inevitable conclusion. As the girls venture further up the Rock, impervious to Edith's screeching imperatives, we move to the fourth and final act of this scene.

'Whatever can those people be doing down there, like a lot of ants? A surprising number of human beings are without purpose. Although it is probable that they are performing some function unknown to themselves.' Marion's observation is inextricably bound up formally with a high-angle long shot of the picnic party from a vantage point at the peak of the Rock. This perspective, which seems most appositely characterised as being marked by free indirect subjectivity (neither that strictly of a character, nor that of the 'objective' camera eye), elides character with environment and, as such, complicates the supposed centrality of a purely human perspective. From this position, Marion sees anew – by looking askance – what was obscured from view at the base of the Rock: that there is as much or as little purpose and order to human life as there is to the life forms to which humans remain ignorant, and that

nature – ultimately – is in control. This vantage point works to deflate Edith's grandiloquent earlier statement that they might be the 'only living creatures in the whole world' (a point of view which the film itself, in fact, treats with bathos throughout). A tracking shot that marries Marion's perspective to that of Irma and Miranda renders clear that all three are now imbricated in this metaphysical frame of reference.

Moreover, Miranda's esoteric statement that 'everything begins and ends at exactly the right time and place' seems to imply a form of knowledge belying her schoolgirlish self, which is to say that this insight comes from beyond her and that they are, indeed, performing some function that remains *unknown to themselves*. The recurring reverse shot of the Rock's face 'looking back' now takes on renewed significance within the context of the girls fulfilling a purpose to which they have remained largely ignorant (a purpose that re-emerges sonically in the earthquake's timbre). What *Picnic* implies through its very form here is a *return* to the earth from which, elementally, all human life comes into being and on which it inevitably meets its end. The earth's resonance seems to draw the girls into slumber, a state from which they only partially awake in order seemingly to ramble oneirically into oblivion. A further allusion is drawn to the earlier picnic scene in which ants consume the Valentine's Day cake; here, the girls' feet and hands are rendered as a form of still life observed and overtaken by animal and insect life. These moments are strangely peaceful; only Edith's high-pitched scream, further heightened and echoed by Smeaton's score, returns us to the terror of the unfolding moment. The protracted pace is suddenly ruptured by a sharply mechanical zoom into Edith's terrified face as she registers the passing of her friends into the unknown, and which is compounded further by an extreme long shot (taken from a helicopter) that registers her hurried and frightful descent from the Rock. As if to ally this disaster directly with the subsequent downfall of Mrs Appleyard and her college, the action cross-cuts to her waiting in her study under a portrait of Queen Victoria; time may have stopped 'dead' at the Rock, but by all measurement of her insistently ticking clock, the picnic party is drawing perilously close to being late to return to the sanctuary of her 'care'; and since the world outside her college for young ladies is clearly – in Appleyard's view – not only dangerous but a potential sink of iniquity, she already intuits something must have gone very wrong indeed back at the Rock; although she cannot yet know that it foretells the obliteration of her own world.

3 Quite Intact: The Male Imaginary
and Courtly Love

One of the taglines used to promote *Picnic* upon its release was
'a recollection of evil'; but what precisely is the nature of this 'evil'
or harm, and by whom is it being recollected? Why would Cliff
Green, *Picnic*'s screenwriter, repeatedly refer to the film as a *murder
mystery* and implicate the character of Michael (the film's ineffectual,
foppish 'hero') in the disappearance and presumed death of these
young women?[65] Ostensibly, these claims help to frame *Picnic* within
the genre of the horror-thriller film; moreover, the tired trope of
'beautiful young women in peril' is a worryingly abiding motif within
visual culture at large deployed to pull in and partially satisfy the
most salacious of appetites. Yet this reading of *Picnic* intimates a far
more disturbing, intangible reality that is present within the film's
very form: the obsessional nature of desire, and the role that beauty
plays within violent fantasy. This is, in part, a tale of male sexualised
violence: whether it is enacted or remains imagined on the level of
the narrative within *Picnic* is (at least as far as I am concerned) of
negligible relevance, for violence is inseparable from its form, and
thus overdetermines its portrayal of the female body – after all, one
need not be a film scholar to isolate the excessive nature of *Picnic*'s
rendering of 'femininity'. As for Michael, a young man so fiercely
intent on saving these young women from seeming oblivion, I must
speak plainly: there are reasons why women are told to be wary of
'gentlemen' who wish to rescue them from all manner of threat,
especially at nightfall. Which is also to say that the shadows of
veneration and love are degradation and hatred.[66]

It is the central contention of work by scholars such as Harriet
Wild, Douglas Keesey and Jonathan Rayner that *Picnic* in both
its form and content is predicated on the notion of courtly love.[67]

We understand this tradition as a literary one dating back to the eleventh and twelfth centuries, which was notably prevalent in France, Germany and England. Yet it is also important that we conceive of it as both a social practice, and a peculiarly psychological predisposition or predilection. Of distinct relevance to *Picnic* are three facets: the highly deliberate invocation of an obstacle between the lover and the beloved, so as to bar physical consummation or satisfaction; the sublimation of sexual impulses so as to amplify and refine love's 'nobler sensibilities'; and the elevation of the beloved to an inaccessible archetype of immortal beauty, unsullied purity and eternal femininity (**W**oman). Of cardinal importance to the latter is the evisceration from female experience of lived, embodied reality and personal characteristics, as well as the abnegation of appetites, drives and – of course – intellectual pursuits. The courtly muse is a perfect, pristine container and vessel. In and of herself, she simply does not exist beyond being a rarefied figment of the male imaginary. Courtly love functions through a studied fixation on beauty to the point of fetishisation; in its dogged pursuit of a pure aestheticism, it works both to suspend and to mortify desire (that is, life). It is for this very reason that Jacques Lacan describes this manifestation of courtly love through sublimation as 'a zone of encroachment of death upon life'.[68] This curious, romanticised perspective serves both to suffocate whomever is held within its spellbound grip *and* the object of this painfully affected stance, thus reducing all experience to a kind of perpetual living death. Representation of the beloved, as such, is finely calibrated so as to cover over, or deny fleshy, corporeal materiality. In fact, Lacan, once again, remarks that beauty works to disguise the truth of human existence.[69] Beauty is, in fact, a screen – the sole purpose of which is to obscure our view of reality.

Objectification is not only the logical consequence of this predisposition: it is its very foundation. Evidently, to focus resolutely on a purely aesthetic or superficial dimension of someone's personhood is to extend little care or compassion towards their lived reality. In fact, it is a predominant element of misogyny – and

a notable feature of many films in the so-called 'cinematic canon'.
It also precipitates, in terms of courtly love, a 'division between
beauty as form and perfection versus sex as material and base' by
which young womanhood, in particular, is idealised as the province
of innocence and innate goodness. The cultural correlate is a form
or representation that posits girlhood as angelic, finely featured,
ethereal, delicate and – above all – white.[70] Beauty must not be
sullied by sexual drives and urges by either party (lover or beloved).
If courtly love entails the elevation of mere mortal women to
Woman so as to hinder any possibility of viewing her as a desiring
individual in and of herself, it also casts her as a self-denying figure
who is 'anorexic, sickly, pale, not of this world ... [and] more dead
than alive'.[71] It is, in other words, an elaborate fantasy: a cultural
construct designed to prevent any confrontation with reality (which
is not to say that we do not powerfully internalise these ideas and
images – clearly, this has extremely damaging consequences for
young women).

Whilst *Picnic* from the outset conveys a knowingly
aestheticised, dematerialised vision of girlhood on the cusp of
womanhood, this *mise en scène* is compounded by focalisation
(namely, Michael's point of view); and it is his perspective, standing
in for that of the film itself, which works to cleave the girls to a
specifically feminine iconicity and to ensure their transformation – in
particular, that of Miranda – into an opulent unreality. The lavish
appeal of *Picnic* is, without doubt, in large part dependent on its
extravagant rendering of white girlhood as arcane, delicate and
ultimately untouchable (which is also to say that the film functions
through unattainable and overtly false imagery). It is Michael's point
of view that draws Miranda into her slow-motion leap towards
the unknown, a device which works to distil her embodied reality
into a romanticised vision of eternal and radiant girlhood. It is his
overwrought imagination that renders her as a swan – a trope of
European folklore that works to braid beauty with tragedy, such
that even a young woman's death is taken from her (she lives on,

OUT-TAKE FROM ORIGINAL NEGATIVE

A Dream Within a Dream: The Making of 'Picnic at Hanging Rock' (2004)

immortalised, in resplendent, sublime beauty – as, in other words, Art). In a scene that was wisely cut from the final version of the film, Miranda appears to Michael as Botticelli's Venus – her nakedness both concealed and yet heightened by gold-flecked paint. These are all highly inventive ways of making her utterly inaccessible as a person.[72]

As we have seen, *Picnic*'s 'soft' aesthetic is, in part, created by the use of a piece of dyed wedding veil placed directly over the camera lens, but what might the psychological purpose of this device be? Harriet Wild notes that

this technique employs, literally, another 'layer of love' – a formal, ritualized acknowledgment of love that can be understood as a form of suturing between the diegetic world ... the apparatus of the camera and lastly the viewer: a 'marriage' of cinematic engagement.[73]

The film does work to draw us, as viewers, further into this rarefied cinematic world by implicitly allying us to Michael's point of view and, by extension, his desire to solve 'the mystery'. The veil is both that which symbolises the obstruction we face in trying to fathom these events and in trying to reach Miranda (who comes to stand in for all the lost girls), as well as that which is a predicate to casting these young women as mythical, all-knowing, luminous creatures.

Accessibility, after all, would render them human and as merely mortal flesh – destined for unremarkable dust like the rest of us. Earlier, when I said *Picnic* is structured formally around a double manoeuvre of acknowledgment and denial which creates a sustained ambivalence that defines its emotional impact as an experience, I meant precisely this: that the viewer wishes to 'penetrate' the mystery of the Rock and, by extension, of these girls, and yet we never *really* wish for the film to dispel its own myth-making. To draw back the curtain is to reveal ugly – and often banal – realities. Michael does not *really* want to attain Miranda: if he did, it would spell the death of his desire (such is, usually, the effect of reality on fanciful imagination). It is telling, as Keesey notes, that he loses consciousness when he is on the point of actually 'rescuing' Miranda from her fate on the Rock.[74] His singular relationship to Irma is also indicative of this. Once she returns – miraculously 'intact' – from the Rock, the generic tropes of romance would dictate that a relationship should bloom between Irma and her 'hero', bound as they are together by apparent triumph over adversity. It is clear that Michael is aware that this is the role into which he is being propelled; tellingly, his 'vigil' at her bedside is mediated through a white, net-like, veil (otherwise known as a prosaic mosquito net) through which she resembles the archetypal 'sleeping princess' waiting to be stirred from slumber.

Yet Michael understands that there is no possibility of rescuing Irma from her nightmare – she may have been returned to him 'intact', but he knows that something has happened to her up there which is beyond his comprehension. She has been irrevocably altered for all time, and in that sense, she can never be returned. She is not an impeccable, spotless screen onto which he can project his phantasies. As such, that veil may signify a desperate attempt to turn her into something she can never actually be to him: in other words, it symbolises a psychological mechanism.

Irma's curse is her experience and knowledge, her embodiment as a young woman who stands before Michael asking to be seen as real. Several scenes detail their failed courtship, culminating in Michael's absence at the family dinner table – the traditional site of proposal or announcement of an engagement to be married. As such, Weir's decision to cut these scenes from the director's version seems misguided, for it misses the fundamental psychological aspect of both

the central male protagonist *and* the film itself: that to become an object of desire, a young woman cannot exist. Absenting these scenes with Irma from the director's cut renders Michael's motivations wholly inexplicable, for inaccessibility, absence, is the vital catalyst for his desire. Notably, Miranda and Irma offset one another within *Picnic*'s narrative. Irma, with her chestnut hair and enquiring gaze, comes to embody a form of experience and knowledge that is perceived to be worldly and dangerous in a woman; we last see her in *Picnic* marked out in red attire, her mere presence seeming to induce a violent hysteria in the other girls at Appleyard College. Conversely, Miranda – whom Sara tells us is the repository of an arcane and secret knowledge: 'Miranda knows things' – must embody the contradictions which patriarchal society tends to project onto the female form. She is at once virginal, pristine and pure, and yet foretells of death and the inexorable passage of time ('I won't be here much longer'); she is seemingly the embodiment of youth and girlhood, whilst also appearing to be older and wiser than those around her; her appearance is intricately codified as both innocent and sexual. It is significant that the actress originally cast to play Miranda, Ingrid Mason, was replaced by Anne Lambert because, visually, she could not convey this ambivalent duality; she appeared to be *too* young, which suggests that it is *the cusp* between adolescence and adulthood – the ambiguity of that liminal moment – that is essential to this particular sexual fantasy of transgression (tempered, notoriously, by plausible 'deniability'). As such, the part of Miranda required an ability to function as a holding space for inherently patriarchal projections and phantasies – a highly skilled performance grounded in vacancy, negativity and absence. That is, a performance of femininity is – necessarily so – a performance of a performance. *Picnic* seems to tell us that in order to desire a young woman in this way, one must kill her – for this kind of objectification, this vitiation of selfhood, this rendering of the female body as merely symbolic *is* a form of violence – a violence endemic, *in my view*, to the majority of dominant forms of cinematic representation. *Picnic*

exposes this through its very form. If this is Michael's recollection of events, we as viewers are also implicated, by extension, in this 'evil' that is brought out into the light. Michael is wounded by the loss of Miranda and compelled in his mind to keep revisiting the site of his trauma, perhaps wholly unaware of his complicity; for we should surely not be so perplexed as to why a young woman might choose to walk out of the frame of a narrative that denies her – and quite literally so – a point of view, which compels her into a position of intolerable subjugation and abnegation in order to shore up male desire, and which forces her to bear the burden of iconicity.

Á l'ombre des jeunes filles en fleurs: from Pre-Raphaelite portraiture to David Hamilton

Marek Haltof notes that the characterisation of young womanhood in *Picnic* closely resembles that of Pre-Raphaelite nineteenth-century portraiture by artists such as Edward Burne-Jones, Dante Gabriel Rossetti, John Everett Millais and Arthur Hughes;[75] he contends further that this might explain why some critics, such as David Myers, whom he quotes, argue that *Picnic* feels like watching 'a male voyeur's nostalgia-trip to a sexual utopia for neo-Victorian necrophiliacs'.[76] Whilst this latter assessment is clearly meant to be taken in spirited humour, it identifies several essential elements of the film's delineation of the female form; first, that *Picnic* clearly does invoke the Pre-Raphaelite fascination with themes of sexuality, constraint, power and death which offended those denizens intent on upholding Victorian notions of feminine propriety; second, that as in Pre-Raphaelite portraiture, female transgression and passionate display is always met with violent riposte. It is notable, after all, that many of these images centre on women in ecstatic rapture at the moment of death, and further that a feminised death in this context is nearly always a 'beautiful' death. As for the 'neo-Victorian necrophiliac', he accords rather too well with our courtly lover.

I do not demur with the assessment that *Picnic* broadly is as much an homage to Pre-Raphaelite portraiture as it is to the Heidelberg school of Impressionism, but its more direct and openly avowed influence is the 'softcore' photography of David Hamilton. There is undoubtedly evident nostalgia in both of these forms of portraiture – though set apart by over a century of artistic momentum – for a past that is, in fact, a fiction of the artist's imagination. Yet whereas this past is embodied in that of women clearly enacting a mythical or folkloric role in Pre-Raphaelite images, Hamilton's photographs locate this queasy longing for a contradictory sexualised, Edenic innocence in evidently young, pubescent female bodies (whilst also professing to have ridiculous pretensions to 'high art'). Moreover, the images of the Pre-Raphaelite women were, in part, created deliberately to abrade the cultural codes and conventions of their day in order to provoke conversation about the moralistic constraints placed on women by society, whereas Hamilton's images work to conceal the reality of how young women's bodies are appropriated for cultural and commercial profit with a veneer of halcyon, bucolic, girlish innocence. And yet these photographs are evidently the direct product of a patriarchal culture that grew out of the specific moment of the late 1960s and early 1970s, which sold itself as an idyll of sexual liberation – a slogan which has been used to reframe this period nostalgically as a time of 'innocence' before the revelations of violence, addiction and abuse in the wake of Charles Manson, the Vietnam War and the stark realities of 'drop-out' culture. Rather, this was a time of violent innocence which allowed for the disavowal of lived realities and abuses of power – a kind of bad faith that persists within much of patriarchal visual culture.

It is telling that contemporary publications aimed at men, such as the magazine GQ, have argued openly that the value of these images lies in their 'innocent eroticism', which is conceived of as a panacea for or antidote to our current 'porn age'.[77] This 'nostalgia' is, in reality, a longing for a rapacious male culture centred on the violation of women's bodies in the name of 'free love' – for there is clearly nothing 'innocent' about knowingly perpetuating violence with impunity. Feminist histories have taught us that this was not a 'different time' that adhered to a looser moral code (the laziest of untruths used to shore up an argument that we cannot judge past behaviour within a contemporary context), but rather further subjugation under a different name. Moreover, obfuscation of this motive in the name of artistic licence is all too often used to silence and shame the very women on whose bodies so much of the artistic Western canon hinges. To have one's body appropriated for cultural use is still appropriation – however noble we believe the artistic endeavour to be. The impulse behind Hamilton's 'softcore' images and those of contemporary 'hardcore' is, I contend, exactly the same.[78] In this sense, 'beautiful' Art is patriarchy's fetish – the poor excuse it relies on in order to conceal its often ugly truths. It is notable that these images are devoid of reference to contemporary political issues: for instance, the movements for civil and women's rights, the war in Vietnam, or industrial strikes for workers' rights and access to equal pay. They present an idyllic carapace enabling disavowal and denial of the time of their own making: *they are a screen*. Given this, what can be said of the motivations behind *Picnic*'s lavishly rich aesthetic?

Russell Boyd has spoken at length in interview about the profound influence Hamilton's photographs had on the overarching aesthetic of *Picnic* (his work is as cardinal an influence as the Heidelberg School), especially with regard to the shots of the girls getting ready for the Valentine's Day picnic with which the film opens. He remembers that

Peter and I went through dozens of magazines and he showed me dozens of images ... he wanted all of the opening shots of the girls in their rooms in the morning to be like David Hamilton ... who has these simply magic pictures of girls by windows. He wanted that kind of style early in the film.[79]

The opening five minutes of *Picnic* do seem, to the casual observer, to be graphic matches for Hamilton's images (especially those in his collections *Rêves de jeunes filles* from 1971, and *Les Demoiselles de Hamilton* or *Sisters* from 1972).[80] Indeed, Stella Bruzzi has remarked that this sequence displays 'an excessive fusion of the mechanics of fetishism and the fetishizing potential of the cinematic apparatus'.[81] She has also argued that *Picnic* 'conforms closely to Freud's hugely influential interpretation of fetishism as a male perversion through which the woman becomes a symbol of masculine desire'.[82] I do not disagree with Bruzzi, but I think these elements of *Picnic*'s *mise en scène* are so excessive that they produce their own site of contestation (since the fetish, which enables both acknowledgment and denial, is not a totalising cover or screen and always necessarily malfunctions). As such, I think we miss something of *Picnic*'s rather camp aesthetic if we cannot admit that the film does anything beyond merely hailing and fetishising femininity. I believe the film itself actively encourages the attentive viewer to read against the superficial grain of the image and, thus, to question the basis of its construction qua *mediation of femininity*.[83] There is a rebellious element to these moving images of young women that is entirely lacking in Hamilton's photographs, much as they are clearly a 'problematic' source of inspiration for the film.

Alongside the 'ascent to the Rock' sequence, the opening images of *Picnic* constitute some of its most abidingly memorable and evocative moments for the viewer. The first words we hear in the film – 'what we see and what we seem are but a dream; a dream within a dream' – are used, naturally, to invoke Poe's literary Gothicism and to provoke viewers into questioning the nature of the 'reality' with which the film presents us (perhaps the pretension here is not to Art, but to metaphysics); most profoundly, though, this opening serves to throw into crisis the ontological status of the cinematic image itself: namely, that this film will present us with multiple reframings (dreams within dreams) which, taken together, reveal the inherent instability of the image. If there is no resolution in *Picnic* it is because its constituent parts continually reveal themselves as construction and undermine any pretence to grand narrative – that whole enterprise of Truth-making. This is apparent immediately in its overtly excessive construction of femininity that does not pertain to reality, but rather to multiple cultural references that have sought to define the status of 'womanhood' – whether the film upholds or seeks to deconstruct those points of reference remains a moot point (I concur with the latter). The sequence opens on a close-up shot of Miranda held in profile and repose with her head resting on a white lace pillow; dressed in a delicate muslin gown, she resembles both Millais's *Ophelia* (1852) and the female subject of any number of Victorian commemorative 'death' photographs.

This *mise en scène* of memento mori is offset, however, by the rise and fall of her chest as she breathes, and the gentle, languorous movement of her head as she turns to face the camera. This visual composition, which from the outset juxtaposes stillness with movement (and life with death), intimates both rebellion against any attempt to 'frame', constrict and distil a young woman to some form of definitive essence, *and* the coterminous harm and suffocation of life (of breath) that acquiescence to 'femininity' may cause. *Picnic*, after all, is a film that invites us to determine the 'meaning' of Miranda ('a Botticelli angel') at the very moment in which she recedes from the frame and usurps any attempt to grasp the 'nature' of her being (even that magnifying glass does not help!). Her representation is inherently dual or split in nature. I cannot go so far as to say that *Picnic* stages an overt confrontation with the male gaze, but rather suggest that by compounding it and rendering it so evident as an explicit facet of its own apparent 'visual appeal', it manifests fascination with the female form *as* fetishisation. Moreover, bearing in mind that the fetish serves to cover over a complexity with which one cannot deal or face, the film appears to invite us to read askance, to question what we see, to peel back the surface to what lies behind or beyond it and to ask what the purpose of these images might be.

The ensuing series of shots are explicitly indebted to Hamilton's *jeunes filles*: these girls are framed in profile against the dormitory windows of Appleyard College; they are bathed in sunlight filtered and softened by the lace curtains adorning the windows; and with their long blonde hair and fair complexions, they strongly resemble an archetype – the 'Nordic girl' which Hamilton favoured as a model. Indeed, *Picnic* even in its opening moments draws the viewer's attention towards the very techniques put in service of creating this feminine *mise en scène*, such as the manipulation of light through muslin, lace and gauze. There are multiple elements which underscore the studied artificiality of this scenario and require parsing:

1. There is a stylised emphasis on the accoutrements of feminine grooming and appearance that seems ritualistic in nature as if to foreground femininity *as performance*: namely, that the female rite of passage *requires* transformation of the self.
2. These images oscillate between themes of release and confinement, an effect which recontextualises the somewhat hackneyed image of a woman before a window as a melodramatic trope that suggests isolation and restraint within the domestic sphere.
3. Tightly laced corsetry and the refraction of mirror images both serve to emphasise and problematise themes of suffocation and

objectification – that is, the film itself makes clear that to become a 'young lady' requires a (literal) diminishment of one's body and self-determination by acquiescing to external frames of reference. The perfect feminine shape is not only the effect of self-abnegating discipline, it is also the result of painful artifice (those creaking sounds are torturous).

4. This opening sequence is overtly sapphic in tone given that these young women are declaring their adoration for one another (although admittedly there is something rather ludicrous about these declarations).[84]

5. It is quite clear that Sara Waybourne is, in fact, in love with Miranda and it is her gaze which complicates the specularisation of Miranda as an object of desire within this scenario.

6. A floral motif is introduced already within this opening section which serves to liken the girls metaphorically not only to 'buds' coming into 'full bloom' (as Hamilton interprets the meaning of *jeunes filles*), but also to hothouse flowers (Appleyard College, like a greenhouse, being a place of artificial generation), plucked and preserved (in a press, yet another form of suffocation) before decay sets in.

As such, the film itself seems to draw attention to both the cruelty and diminishments enfranchised by educational establishments intent on walking young girls into the renunciations occasioned by womanhood (for which male admiration is the doubtful prize and reward). It also strategically draws attention to itself as a document of preservation – an argument which, interestingly enough, Hamilton's staunchest defenders have also used to shore up his work as Art.[85] *Picnic*'s interpretation of the *jeune fille* is rather an individual who is deracinated, suffocated and made fit for purpose within a society that delimits and defines the possibilities of her existence: as a beautiful – but dead – object, *as a Woman* before

Directed by
PETER WEIR

having a chance to become a person. It is not, to my mind, accidental that the credit 'directed by Peter Weir' appears superimposed over an over-the-shoulder shot of Marion placing a white rose within a flower press and then gently working its screws into hermetic closure. There is also something markedly different in nature about *Picnic*'s girls than those caught within Hamilton's frame: they wear glasses (that most abiding of motifs used to suggest women who look out at the world and possess knowledge), they share secrets with one another to which we are not party, they laugh and joke with one another, and play pranks on their teachers.

Instrumental to this sequence is a composite use of mirror images; within the same frame, Miranda's reflected image is doubly refracted, which effects visually a stop-gap that complicates our relationship to her as object of desire through multiple reframings. Her *to-be-looked-at-ness* is not concealed within or explicitly motivated by the narrative;[86] rather, it is compounded and heightened so as to pose the question of femininity through production design. And whereas Freud concluded that women were incapable of solving the 'riddle' of femininity, since they themselves 'are the problem', *Picnic* seems to suggest that the problem may well be the obsessional nature of patriarchal logic itself.[87] The riddle of femininity is overtly posed here as a false problem, a construct, which is subsequently

imposed on the minds and bodies of young women as the harbingers of all that is lacking and inadequate so as to shore up masculinity all the better. As Jonathan Rayner argues, *Picnic* constructs 'an eroticized image of a woman, created by a male and reflecting a male-oriented institution (Victorian society of the cinema)', which it then purposefully distances us from so that this image is 'lost … from the voyeur and understood only *on the level of image*. The male, and the camera, lose sight of the female when they leave the constriction of the societal construct' (emphasis mine).[88] Rayner identifies something crucial about the feminised images with which *Picnic* presents us: that we are expected to read them *at the level of the image*, not to 'justify' them in terms of the narrative, since the film itself refuses all such attempts at rendering the girls *meaningful*.

As such, what *Picnic* emphasises is the ontological instability of the image or any given representation: that there is a necessary gap between signifier and signified. In this image of Miranda before a 'looking glass', we do not merely revel in the appearance of a beautiful young woman who cannot return our gaze. *Picnic* refutes such simplicity of interpretation. To be clear, I am not arguing that *Picnic* stages a radical feminist intervention into the paradigm of the cinematic male gaze – patently it does not do so – but I do believe that these images are far more complex than merely constituting an invitation to take unadulterated pleasure in looking (which, I am quite sure, many viewers do feel, but if this is *all* they are doing and feeling they have, as far as I am concerned, missed most of what is actually unfolding on screen). So what do we have before us here? Initially, Miranda faces her own reflection in a bevelled table mirror as she brushes her hair. This image within an image is contextualised by the large dresser mirror placed behind the tabletop mirror. Caught within this frame is the reflection of Miranda looking at her own image, the reflection of the back of the smaller mirror and Sara as she faces away from the larger mirror. It is the position of the camera to the left of the frame which creates the effect of the 'free-floating' oval-shaped image of Miranda within the frame. This image stages

yet another version of what John Berger, writing in 1972, argues is
the spectacle of a woman joining in with 'the spectators of herself', by
which she is typically pictured naked and with a mirror in her hand;
he comments that

you painted a naked woman because you enjoyed looking at her, you put
a mirror in her hand, and you called the painting *Vanity*, thus morally
condemning the woman whose nakedness you had depicted for your own
pleasure. *The real function of the mirror was otherwise. It was to make the woman
connive in treating herself as, first and foremost, a sight.* (emphasis mine)[89]

Of course, Miranda is not naked here but we have as our intertextual
reference point Hamilton's photographs of young girls in a state of
undress (strategically clothed nakedness) with which these opening
images comprise a partial graphic match (the visual equivalent of a
half-rhyme).

This cinematic *mise en abyme*, which already gestures towards
the 'dream within a dream' that is the very substance of the film,
serves to foreground visually the terms and motivations of its own
making. Namely, that the female rite of passage addressed here works
to corral lived existence and image together so that the meaning of
womanhood is effected through – in fact is strictly bound up with –
adhering to a highly specific kind of representation. Moreover, this
image is extraneous, it comes to us from elsewhere (from outside).
It determines a form of self-alienation particular to the experience of
many young women. This is evident in the displacement of her own
reflection; the effect of this within the frame is to isolate her virtual
image via a perspective that is only afforded *by the camera* itself.
As such, this single shot dramatises *before a mirror* (a space beset by
psychoanalytic meaning and interpretation) the split between ideal
ego (as venerated, false image) and the complex social positioning
of the ego ideal (the cultural approbation of such an image). Within
the opening moments of the film, then, we as viewers are subtly
implicated within the social position of the ego ideal. We are the

people *for whom* young girls might identify with an image which remains extraneous to them because they know it is one sanctioned as correct or pleasing by society at large. The film works to place itself within the context of being what feminist theorist Teresa de Lauretis has termed a 'technology of gender'.[90] What complicates this scenario further is that the lover's look, the gaze to which Miranda is beholden here, is not merely that of the camera (of the technical, mechanical apparatus coded as male), but that of its stand-in: the young, awkward and abused orphan Sara Waybourne. Sara is held in the centre of the frame; she is the epicentre of this complex refraction of the cinematic gaze and it is to her that Miranda, in turn, looks and expresses affection.

Of great import is the Valentine's Day card displayed (amongst other affectionate missives) on the dresser in front of Miranda. The front cover depicts a white swan, framed within a border of ornate doily and glued to the front of mint-green card. This love note is from Sara to Miranda. Before Miranda is transformed into a swan by the male imaginary (via Michael's gaze), she is *imaged* as such by Sara, an obscure girl to whom nobody except Miranda seems to pay much notice, who suffers ghastly abuse at the hands of Mrs Appleyard and Miss Lumley (fittingly, the mistress of physical education and deportment), and whose abject misery resulting in

suicide is dismissed. This is to say that the relationship between
Miranda and Sara is evidently one of love: they see one another in a
way that is, in fact, almost unique to lovers. Sara knows that Miranda
possesses knowledge well beyond the bounds of what Appleyard
College has inculcated in her; she also knows that Miranda is fated
for another kind of destiny. Miranda sees that Sara is someone
who needs to be seen, who is so perilously close to the verge of
disappearance precisely because nobody apparently cares for her.
It is Miranda's solicitous and loving gaze which, in essence, keeps
her alive. So when Miranda reminds her that she must 'learn to love
somebody else' because she is not going to be 'here for much longer',
Sara intuits manifold layers of meaning in this statement – and we do
so as well by identifying with her. Physically, Miranda is on the cusp
of womanhood and is being walked into a station in life befitting of
a 'young lady': a situation beyond her control; she is also indicating
that their kind of love is not sanctioned beyond this particular frame
and moment and that if Sara is to survive, she must also learn to
diminish the reality of her sexual and amorous inclinations.[91]

   That this speech is delivered via a cut to close-up through which
Miranda's reflected image is held within the centre of the frame also
intimates the extent to which she knows this future to be one of
confinement and delimitation. She will exist no longer as herself, but

as the image of womanhood society has deemed appropriate. Like that swan, caught within a florid and ornate frame and turned into a decorative image (a Victorian bookmark, a collector's item), Miranda understands that she is being called upon to taper and contract herself into the narrow confines of feminine duty. And yet, her speech clearly has a third meaning. Crucially, our access to Miranda's image here is through what the camera sees. We do not see what she sees; we are not transported into her point of view. If she remains opaque and inaccessible, there is also something highly subversive in this. She retains the ability to think and to see otherwise. She retains the ability to walk away from this hermetic, staid, Victorian world and its values and to disappear from view entirely.

Conclusion: Girls on the Verge; Femininity and Hysteria

To the contemporary reader, it may seem perverse that I believe *Picnic*'s radical site of potentially feminist contestation may lie in its portrayal of hysteria; yet as Elaine Showalter reminds us: '[h]ysteria concerns feminists because the label has always been used to discredit women's political protest.'[92] Hysteria has been recuperated by feminist and psychoanalytic scholars in particular (Hélène Cixous, Catherine Clément, Luce Irigaray) as a phenomenon which manifests the oppression of women's voices and sexuality through embodiment. That is, as Cixous et al. conceive of it, hysteria – after Lacan, who conflates hysteria and femininity – is the site from which femininity 'speaks back' to the Master in order to challenge his most deeply held assumptions about womanhood (to un-master that which seeks culturally to confine women, and to name that which harms them). It poses the perennial 'problem' or 'riddle' of femininity as a social construct expressed somatically through a body that 'speaks' its history in symptoms. Showalter reminds us that

[n]ineteenth-century hysterical women suffered from the lack of a public voice to articulate their economic and sexual oppression, and their symptoms – mutism, paralysis, self-starvation, spasmodic seizures – seemed like bodily metaphors for the silence, immobility, denial of appetite, and hyper-femininity imposed on them by their societies.[93]

Moreover, she reminds us that hysteria, by its very nature, is a *mimetic* disorder, expressing repression and abject distress through what is deemed socially legitimate within a given historical context and thus what is already codified and *able or available to be read*.[94]

Of course, it does not follow that this narrative of the body will be read incisively or even sensitively – Freud's failed analysis of Ida Bauer (Dora) being merely one infamous example. Crucially, Showalter emphasises that epidemics of hysteria often crest and peak at the turn of a century or during intense moments of social upheaval and political change. Hysterics, then, also act as conduits for the anxieties and social precarity of the time in which they are living, bodying forth what remains unspoken, unacknowledged and refused by wider, socially approbated political discourse. In her paradigm-shifting study, Juliet Mitchell has persuasively argued that hysteria does not merely throw the supposition of subjectivity into crisis, but problematises the very notion of social organisation. She argues that the hysteric does not simply ask 'who am I?', but rather demands '*where* am I?' That is, the female hysteric is embroiled in a complex negotiation of women's status within society, since, for Mitchell, the hysteric is an individual who rejects 'displacement' within social relations, and in doing so refuses to assimilate the social position handed to her; as a result, she argues, the hysteric experiences displacement as 'an ineradicable trauma'.[95] Under both of these accounts, the hysteric is not purely a victim of patriarchal coercion, she is also someone who takes up the rebellious stance of speaking truth to power in the only language available to her (for if one is continually met with a stubborn refusal to listen, one is forced to find other means). I recognise fully that this is a skewed bargain, that proverbial poisoned chalice which harbours the potential for obscurity at best and self-obliteration at worst. It is, however, the *symbolic* dimension of hysteria that interests me with regard to *Picnic*, the diegetic environment of which is saturated with both anxiety and desire. I am preoccupied with the notion of *Picnic* as a film that centres directly on what it might mean to live within a narrative that is not of one's own making and the violence that inevitably erupts from this. As such, hysteria is woven into its very form – a form which strains to contain the excessive nature of its own emotional landscape.

Davina Quinlivan has aptly noted that this is a film in which the female characters write themselves out of a narrative into which they refuse to be made to fit. They constitute, she argues, 'the vanishing point within patriarchal cinema, as Dora is a vanishing point in Freud's case study'.[96] I cannot brook readings of *Picnic* which overdetermine the 'phallic' nature of the Rock, offset by its 'yonic' caves. It seems to me that the girls discover something far more subversive and disruptive than a mere potential initiation into 'carnal knowledge' up there on the Rock. We are, after all, meant to find faintly ridiculous the lubricious obsession shared by doctors and school mistresses alike with the girls' bodily integrity ('she's quite intact'). For this is a system of education that is predicated on disciplining the female body into acceptable forms (a sanctioned form of interference, if you will). As such, they read the female body for evidence in all the wrong ways (a Freudian error), and in doing so miss their fundamental complicity within a system that performs daily acts of attrition and violence on the female body in the name of (re)education. That penultimate shot of Sara before her body is discovered by the gardener after her suicide remains shocking for a reason. Distilled into a single image of a child strapped to a posture board, abandoned and whimpering in pain, is the brutality of a feminine rite of passage that works to diminish the strength and will

of a girl into the 'pleasing' (correct) form of a young lady. If Irma's visit induces in the other girls a ferocious hysteria, it is because she has learned another form of knowledge – not necessarily sexual in nature, but subversive of and potentially destructive to an existing social order which is slowly and inexorably brutalising them. Their collective demand that she '*tell*' of this knowledge spells the point at which Appleyard College – that monument to colonial authority, pomposity and arrogance, and by extension the delusional narrative its matriarch has spun around it – begins to unravel and crumble. In fact, we grow to understand that Appleyard herself is extremely

psychologically ill. *Picnic* is not a film which shies away from cruelty: it forces us to *recollect* and to *confront* evil. For it is there for us to see, not in the recesses and the shadows, but within the light of day. This is, finally, the truth of *Picnic*'s terror.

There are three female film-makers who have seen this in *Picnic* and understand the film to be, at its very core, about violence wrought on the female body. Carol Morley's *The Falling* (2014), Lucile Hadzihalilovic's *Innocence* (2004) and Sofia Coppola's utterly exceptional debut film *The Virgin Suicides* (1999) stand collectively as both paean and testament to the enduring cultural power and

The Falling (2014)

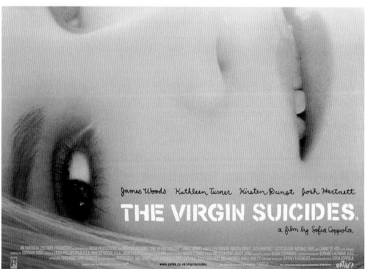

Innocence (2004); *The Virgin Suicides* (1999)

influence of *Picnic* as a haunting, deeply unsettling cinematic experience. These are films which radically reconfigure the female rite of passage as one beset by viciousness, indifference and sadism; more subversively, these films argue that this is a form of deliberate cruelty promulgated by bastions of patriarchal culture, such as a gendered educational system, and even the nuclear family. They grapple directly with the consequences of making young women bear the unendurable weight of what I have referred to here as the 'burden of iconicity'. They tell us that we should never be surprised to discover that refusal, silence, violence and death come as mutual ripostes to systems designed to walk young women into subjugation. They demand we prise open this beautiful veneer to expose the pitiless reality lying just beneath the surface, waiting to be brought out into the light. These images may be necessarily fictitious in nature, but what they ask us to reckon with is very real indeed … perhaps this is why so many of us are still being haunted by *Picnic at Hanging Rock*. Will you answer its call?

Notes

1 See in particular Susan Dermody and Elizabeth Jacka, *The Screening of Australia: Anatomy of a National Cinema, Vol. 2* (Sydney: Currency Press, 1988).
2 See David Castell, 'Weir, Weird, and Weirder Still: The Riddle of Hanging Rock', in John C. Tibbetts (ed.), *Peter Weir: Interviews* (Jackson: University Press of Mississippi, 2014 [1976]), pp. 79–80.
3 See the documentary *A Dream Within a Dream: The Making of 'Picnic at Hanging Rock'* (dir. Mark Hartley, 2004).
4 Brian McFarlane, 'The Australian Literary Adaptation: An Overview', *Literature/Film Quarterly* vol. 21, no. 2 (1993), p. 91.
5 Peter Weir states that film critic Philip French said this of the film (see *A Dream Within a Dream*). He also restates this in 2008 (see 'DVD Reviews', *Guardian*, 6 July 2008).
6 Patricia Lovell, interview by Martha Ansara, 2 July 1993. Accessed by author on 23 February 2021 from the National Film and Sound Archive of Australia. Permission granted by Martha Ansara and Jennifer Lovell. However, I have not been able to ascertain this fact from anyone else involved in the film's making.
7 Cliff Green, interview by Ina Bertrand, 2007. Accessed by author on 25 February 2021 from the NFSA. Permission granted by the NFSA (licensed agreement for public use); and Lovell, interview by Ansara.
8 Lovell, interview by Ansara.
9 See Jonathan Rayner, *The Films of Peter Weir* (London and New York: Cassell, 1998), p. 61.
10 *A Dream Within a Dream*.

11 Patricia Lovell, archival interview, 1975. Interviewer not specified, but stored under file 430554 at the NFSA. Permission granted by Jennifer Lovell.
12 Patricia Lovell, *No Picnic: An Autobiography* (Sydney: Pan Macmillan Australia, 1995), p. 140.
13 Ibid., p. 147.
14 Ibid., p. 148.
15 Ibid., p. 151.
16 Green, interview by Bertrand.
17 *A Dream Within a Dream*.
18 Lovell, *No Picnic*, p. 152.
19 Ibid., p. 153.
20 Ibid., p. 154.
21 Green, interview by Bertrand.
22 Lovell, archival interview; Lovell, interview by Ansara.
23 See Lovell, archival interview.
24 See Lovell, interview by Ansara.
25 Lovell, *No Picnic*, p. 169.
26 Archival interview footage with Joan Lindsay in *A Dream Within a Dream*.
27 Ibid.
28 After Lindsay's death, John Taylor released the infamous 'lost' and final chapter of the book. Chapter eighteen, as it has come to be known, offers an explanation of the narrative's mysterious events via recourse to a fourth dimension of reality in which Greta McCraw, the mathematics teacher, reappears first as a 'clown', and then as a crab, and proceeds to usher two of the girls through a portal and into an alternate reality.
29 See Lovell, interview by Ansara.
30 Russell Boyd, interview by Frank Heymans, 25 June 2010. Accessed by author on 25 February 2021 from the NFSA. Permission granted by the NFSA.

31 Lovell, *No Picnic*, p. 137.

32 Helen Morse, interview by Margaret Leask, 2015. Accessed by author on 23 February 2021 from the NFSA. Permission granted by Morse.

33 Jan Dawson, 'Picnic Under Capricorn', *Sight and Sound* vol. 45, no. 2 (1976), p. 83.

34 Douglas Keesey, 'Weir(d) Australia: *Picnic at Hanging Rock* and *The Last Wave*', *LIT: Literature, Interpretation, Theory* vol. 8, nos. 3–4 (1998), p. 331.

35 Lovell, *No Picnic*, p. 138.

36 See Boyd, interview by Heymans.

37 Tibbetts, 'I Am Your Eyes', p. 217.

38 See Boyd, interview by Heymans.

39 Tibbetts, 'I Am Your Eyes', pp. 215–16.

40 See Boyd, interview by Heymans.

41 Tibbetts, 'I Am Your Eyes', p. 207.

42 Weir states in interview that he wanted the music to give the impression that 'we are dealing with the old gods' (*A Dream Within a Dream*).

43 Saviour Catania, 'The Hanging Rock Piper: Weir, Lindsay, and the Spectral Fluidity of Nothing', *Literature/Film Quarterly* vol. 40, no. 2 (2012), pp. 84–95, 87.

44 Dawson, 'Picnic Under Capricorn', p. 83.

45 Weir quoted in Rayner, *Films of Peter Weir*, p. 69.

46 The Heidelberg School is often dated by art historians as extraordinarily brief (1885–90).

47 On 3 June 1992, the Australian government acknowledged through its High Court that the legal jurisdiction of *terra nullius* should never have been applied to Australia. In effect, the Australian government recognised that the Aboriginal and Torres Strait Islander populations have a right to the land that was taken from them by the white European settler population, that this right legally preceded the arrival of European settlers, and that it remains their right to this day. The government resolved that reparation must be made to the Aboriginal people of Australia in light of this ruling.

48 Laura Mulvey, 'Visual Pleasure and Narrative Cinema', *Screen* vol. 16, no. 3 (1975), pp. 6–18.

49 See Catania, 'The Hanging Rock Piper', p. 87; and Stephanie Gauper, 'Aborigine Spirituality as the Grounding Theme in the Films of Peter Weir', *Midwest Quarterly* vol. 42, no. 2 (2001), pp. 212–27.

50 Gauper, 'Aborigine Spirituality', p. 213.

51 Susan Sontag, *On Photography* (London: Penguin, 1979), p. 15.

52 Philip Larkin, 'Aubade', in *Collected Poems* (London: Faber & Faber, 2014 [1977]).

53 Sigmund Freud, *The Standard Edition of the Complete Psychological Works of Sigmund Freud*, Vol. XVII (London: The Hogarth Press, 1919), pp. 224–5.

54 Ibid., pp. 225–6.

55 Ibid., p. 241.

56 Stephen Heath, 'Cinema and Psychoanalysis: Parallel Histories', in Janet Bergstrom (ed.), *Endless Night: Cinema and Psychoanalysis, Parallel Histories* (Berkeley: University of California Press, 1999), pp. 25–56, 31.

57 Alison Horbury, 'The Real Gaze in Australian Cinema', *Studies in*

Australasian Cinema vol. 14, no. 3 (2020), pp. 194–214, 208.

58 Ibid.

59 Michael Bliss, *Dreams Within a Dream: The Films of Peter Weir* (Carbondale: Southern Illinois University Press, 2000), p. 52.

60 Elspeth Tilley, 'The Uses of Fear: Spatial Politics in the Australian White-Vanishing Trope', *Antipodes* vol. 23, no. 1 (2009), pp. 33–41, 35.

61 See Jonathan Rayner, 'Gothic Definitions: The New Australian "Cinema of Horrors"', *Antipodes* vol. 25, no. 1 (2011), pp. 91–7.

62 Quoted in Keesey, 'Weir(d) Australia', p. 332.

63 Ibid., p. 333.

64 Pascal Bonitzer, *Décadrages: peinture et cinéma* (Paris: PAH Cinema, 1985).

65 *A Dream Within a Dream*.

66 Douglas Keesey remarks that in *Picnic* 'there are clues suggesting that [Michael] may have raped her [Miranda] … then murdered and buried her to cover up his crime'. See Keesey, 'Weir(d) Australia', p. 333.

67 See Keesey, 'Weir(d) Australia', Rayner, *Films of Peter Weir* and 'Gothic Definitions', and (especially) Harriet Wild, 'Darling Miranda: Courtly Love in *Picnic at Hanging Rock*', *Studies in Australian Cinema* vol. 8, nos. 2–3 (2014), pp. 123–32.

68 Quoted in Bruce Fink, *Lacan on Love: An Exploration of Lacan's Seminar VIII, Transference* (London: Polity, 2016), p. 132.

69 Jacques Lacan, *The Seminar of Jacques Lacan, Book VII: The Ethics of Psychoanalysis (1959–1960)*, ed. J.-A. Miller, trans. R. Grigg (New York: Norton, 1992).

70 See Fink, *Lacan on Love*, p. 129.

71 Ibid., p. 131.

72 Venus is actually Mlle de Poitiers's characterisation of Miranda; yet whilst she is intent on reading her as a 'Botticelli angel', Michael's vision of her here is overtly sexual in nature. Yet Michael professes to find sexual objectification of women vulgar, and is offended by Albert's appraisal of the girls' figures. This excluded image evinces the eroticism that underpins all such images of intricately codified femininity.

73 See Wild, 'Darling Miranda', p. 128.

74 Keesey, 'Weir(d) Australia', p. 336.

75 Marek Haltof, 'The Spirit of Australia in *Picnic at Hanging Rock*: A Case Study in Film Adaptation', *Canadian Review of Comparative Literature* vol. 23, no. 3 (1996), p. 821.

76 Ibid., p. 819.

77 See Perry Hinton, 'Remembrance of Things Past: The Cultural Context and the Rise and Fall in the Popularity of Photographer David Hamilton', *Cogent Arts and Humanities* vol. 3, no. 1 (2016), p. 10.

78 Hamilton was in fact the first choice to direct the *Emmanuelle* film franchise (1974–93), a series of erotic films that progressed from depicting softcore pornography in the 1970s (if one can consider a film depicting sexual assault as such a thing) to hardcore penetrative sex in the 1990s. Hamilton's own work also progressed in a similar fashion, his publication *Private Collection* (1976) marking a falling out of favour due to its increasingly explicit content and a refusal to depict women's faces in favour of focusing on genitalia. Hamilton committed suicide in 2016 after four women he had photographed in the 1970s came forward to accuse him of sexual assault. Despite Hamilton widely claiming he never photographed children, all four women stated they were underage at the time and, moreover, that they were groomed to seek out other girls for him. In 2012, shortly before her death, Sylvia Kristel, the Dutch star of the *Emmanuelle* films, revealed that she had been raped at the age of nine, an event which left her deeply traumatised.

79 See Russell Boyd, interview by Martha Ansara, 15 February 1978.

80 These books sold over one million copies, proving how culturally accepted and resonant they were in the 1970s.

81 See Stella Bruzzi, *Undressing Cinema: Clothing and Identity in the Movies* (London and New York: Routledge, 1997), p. 44.

82 Ibid., p. 37.

83 Between the 1970s and 1990s, Hamilton was the photographer behind the advertising campaign for Nina Ricci's popular fragrance L'Air du Temps. As such, his highly specific mediation of what it means to be a woman (in a patriarchal sense) was harnessed to sell 'femininity' as a brand to women. I believe *Picnic*, in part, reveals and questions this kind of manipulation wrought through images.

84 Notably, Hamilton used sapphic themes in his own work to denote innocence – as a world devoid of the 'penetrative' sexuality of men. Not only does this evince a failure to admit that lesbianism exists – an invisibility perpetrated by patriarchal visual culture at large (unless it recuperates female homosexuality as performance for the male gaze) and all too evident in the misogynist claim 'but what do women do in bed with one another?' – it also signals a wholesale refusal to admit to the reality of his own sexualised violence towards the young women he photographed.

85 See Kenneth Anderson, 'The Remoteness that Betrays Desire', *Times Literary Supplement*, 11 July 1977.

86 Mulvey, 'Visual Pleasure and Narrative Cinema', pp. 6–18.

87 Sigmund Freud, Lecture XXXIII: 'Femininity' (1933), in Leticia Glocer Fiorini and Graciela Abelin-Sas Rose (eds), *On Freud's 'Femininity'* (London: Karnac Books, 2010), pp. 8–31.

88 Rayner, *Films of Peter Weir*, p. 65.

89 John Berger, *Ways of Seeing* (London: Penguin Books, 1972), p. 26.

90 Teresa de Lauretis, *Technologies of Gender: Essays on Theory, Film and Fiction* (Bloomington: Indiana University Press, 1987).

91 For an extensive reading of the depiction of lesbian relationships in *Picnic*, see Sophia Davidson-Gluyas, 'Missing the Lesbian and the Missing Lesbian: A Study of the Forgotten Lesbian in 1970s Australian Cinema', in Graham Willett and Yorick Smaal (eds), *Intimacy, Violence and Activism* (Melbourne: Monash University Publishing, 2013), pp. 90–104.

92 Elaine Showalter, *Hystories: Hysterical Epidemics and Modern Culture* (New York: Columbia University Press, 1997), p. 10.
93 Ibid., pp. 54–5.
94 Ibid., p. 15.
95 Juliet Mitchell, *Mad Men and Medusas: Reclaiming Hysteria and the Effects of Sibling Relations on the Human Condition* (London: Penguin, 2000), p. 323.
96 Davina Quinlivan, 'Her Skin Against the Rocks, the Rocks Against the Sky: Revisiting Weir's *Picnic at Hanging Rock* (1975) After Morley's *The Falling* (2014) and Freud's Fable of Female Hysteria', in Agnieszka Piotrowska and Ben Tyrer (eds), *Femininity and Psychoanalysis: Cinema, Culture, Theory* (London and New York: Routledge, 2019), pp. 37–48, 46.

Credits

Picnic at Hanging Rock
Australia
1975

Directed by
Peter Weir
Screenplay by
Cliff Green
Based on the novel
by Joan Lindsay
Musician (Pan Flute)
Gheorghe Zamfir
**Additional Original
Music Composed by**
Bruce Smeaton
Art Direction by
David Copping
Director of Photography
Russell Boyd
(as Russel Boyd)
Edited by
Max Lemon
**Executive Producer
(South Australian
Film Corporation)**
A. John Graves
(as John Graves)
Executive Producer
Patricia Lovell
Produced by
Hal McElroy
Jim McElroy
Production Company
Picnic Productions
B.E.F. Film Distributors
South Australian Film
Corporation
Australian Film
Commission

B.E.F. Film Distributors
PTY Ltd presents
with the South
Australian Film
Corporation
and the Australian
Film Commission
A McElroy & McElroy
Production
Produced in association
with Patricia Lovell
© 1975 Picnic Production
PTY Ltd

Camera Operator
John Seale
Focus Puller
David Williamson
Clapper Loader
David Foreman
Key Grip
Geordie Dryden
Assistant Grip
Phil Warner
Nature Photography
David Sanderson
Sound Recording
Don Connolly
Boom
Joe Spinelli
Dubbing Editor
Greg Bell
**Assistant Dubbing
Editor**
Sherry Bell
**Artistic Advisor
to Director**
Martin Sharp
1st Assistant Director
Mark Egerton

2nd Assistant Director
Kim Dalton
3rd Assistant Director
Ian Jamieson
Script Consultant
Sidney L. Stebel
(as Sidney Stebel)
Continuity
Gilda Baracchi
Casting
M&L Casting
Consultants
Production Assistant
Steve Knapman
Costume Design by
Judith Dorsman
(as Judy Dorsman)
**Associate Costume
Designer**
Wendy Stites
Wardrobe Assistant
Mandy Smith
Makeup
Liz Michie
(as Elizabeth Mitchie)
Makeup Supervisor
José Luis Pérez
(as Jose Perez)
**Property Buyer/Set
Dresser**
Graham 'Grace' Walker
(as Graham Walker)
**Property Master/
Standby**
Mont Fieguth
(as Monte Fieguth)
**Assistant to the
Art Director**
Christopher Webster

**Assistant to the
Art Department**
Neil Angwin
Construction Manager
Bill Howe
Titles and Opticals
Optical and Graphic
Gaffer
Tony Tegg
Best Boy
Trevor Toune
Electrician
Geoffrey Simpson
Lighting Equipment
Tony Tegg Lighting
Production Secretary
Pom Oliver
Accountant
Joan McIntosh
SAFC Accountant
Phil Smythe
**SAFC Production
Secretary**
Jill Wishart
Still Photography by
David Kynoch
Wrangler
Tom Downer
Assistant Wrangler
Gordon Rayner
Assistant Film Editor
Andre Fleuren
Negative Matcher
Margaret Cardin
Sound Mix
United Sound
Laboratory
Colorfilm (Australia)
PTY Ltd
Camera and Lenses by
Panavision

uncredited
Sound Mixer
Julian Ellingworth
Construction
Herbert Pinter

CAST
Rachel Roberts
Mrs Appleyard
Vivean Gray
Miss Greta McCraw
Helen Morse
Mlle de Poitiers
Kirsty Child
Miss Lumley
**Tony Llewellyn-Jones
(as Anthony
Llewellyn-Jones)**
Tom
Jacki Weaver
Minnie
Frank Gunnell
Mr Whitehead
**Anne-Louise Lambert
(as Anne Lambert)**
Miranda St Clare
Karen Robson
Irma
Jane Vallis
Marion Quade
Christine Schuler
Edith
Margaret Nelson
Sara Waybourne
Ingrid Mason
Rosamund
Jenny Lovell
Blanche
Janet Murray
Juliana

Vivienne Graves
Angela Bencini
Melinda Cardwell
Annabel Powrie
Amanda White
Lindy O'Connell
Verity Smith
Deborah Mullins
Sue Jamieson
Bernadette Bencini
Barbara Lloyd
pupils
Wyn Roberts
Sergeant Bumpher
Kay Taylor
Mrs Bumpher
Garry McDonald
Constable Jones
Martin Vaughan
Ben Hussey
**John Fegan
(as Jack Fegan)**
Dr McKenzie
Peter Collingwood
Colonel Fitzhubert
Olga Dickie
Mrs Fitzhubert
Dominic Guard
Michael Fitzhubert
**John Jarratt
(as John Jarrett)**
Albert Crundall

uncredited
Kevin Gebert
bus driver
Faith Kleinig
cook

Production Details

Made on location at
Hanging Rock, Victoria,
Strathalbyn and
Clare, Marbury School
South Australia and
South Australian Film
Corporation Studios.
35mm
1.66:1
Colour (Eastmancolor)
Running time:
115 minutes
Length: 10,388 feet
MPAA certification
no. 25645

Release Details

Australian premiere on
8 August 1975 in
Adelaide; Australian
theatrical release 1975
by British Empire Films
Australia
UK theatrical release
1976 by G.T.O. Films Ltd